THE QUARTZITE BORDER

Surveying and Marking the North Dakota-South Dakota Boundary

1891-1892

THE QUARTZITE BORDER

Surveying and Marking the North Dakota-South Dakota Boundary 1891-1892

by
GORDON L. ISEMINGER
The University of North Dakota-Grand Forks

The Center for Western Studies
Augustana University
Sioux Falls, South Dakota
2019

Published by the Center for Western Studies
Mailing address: Augustana College, 2001 S. Summit Ave., Sioux Falls, SD 57197
Building address: Fantle Building for the Center for Western Studies, 2121 S. Summit Ave., Sioux Falls, SD 57197
E-mail address: cws@augie.edu
Copies of the current book catalog are available upon request at 605-274-4007 or visit http://www.augie.edu/cws.

The Center for Western Studies (CWS) is an archives, library, museum, publishing house, and educational agency concerned principally with collecting, preserving, and interpreting prehistoric, historic, and contemporary materials that document native and immigrant cultures on the northern prairie-plains. The Center promotes understanding of the region through exhibits, publications, art shows, conferences, and academic programs. It is committed, ultimately, to defining the contribution of the region to American civilization.

ISBN 978-0-931170-40-9
Library of Congress Catalog Card Number 88-71338

Front Cover Photo: Looking into North Dakota at the half-mile monument between miles 285 and 286, south of Hettinger, North Dakota. Photo by author.

Back Cover Photo: Charles H. Bates at the terminal monument, August 1892. South Dakota State Historical Society.

First Edition, First Printing, 1988
Second Printing, with revisions, 2007
Third Printing, 2019
Printed in the United States of America by Anundsen Publishing Company

Preface to the Second Printing

The second printing of *The Quartzite Border: Surveying and Marking the North Dakota-South Dakota Boundary, 1891-1892* nearly twenty years after its first publication will be welcomed by those who have been unable to obtain copies because the book has long been out of print. Few corrections needed to be made to the second printing. One that was made occurs on page 110. Russell E. Kastelle, Registered Land Surveyor, offers a more plausible explanation than my original one for the orientation of Monument 230 as it appears in the accompanying photograph on page 111.

Readers of the second printing must be aware that the condition of the boundary monuments, as described in Chapter 8, for example, was their condition when the author took the photographs to illustrate the 1988 edition. In the years since, some monuments have succumbed to the forces of erosion and the elements. Not a few may have been removed for the convenience of farmers and highway engineers. And, sadly, others have been appropriated by those desiring unique lawn or garden ornaments or unusual mementos. On the other hand, some historically minded citizens have taken pains to protect monuments and, in some cases, have located discarded or buried monuments and set them in what they believed to be their original locations.

Contents

Acknowledgments

I want to thank Ole Breum for introducing me to the quartzite monuments. This study is the product of that introduction. I also want to thank those who read the manuscript and offered helpful suggestions on how to improve it: D. Jerome Tweton, Dan Rylance, Jim Turner, and Russell E. Kastelle.

I also want to acknowledge the kindnesses and assistance extended to me by the staffs at the following places of research: National Archives and Records Service, Washington, D.C.; South Dakota State Historical Society in Pierre; State Historical Society of North Dakota in Bismarck; the Elwyn B. Robinson Department of Special Collections, Chester Fritz Library, University of North Dakota, Grand Forks, North Dakota; Siouxland Heritage Museums, Sioux Falls, South Dakota; Center for Western Studies, Augustana College, Sioux Falls, South Dakota; Pipestone County Historical Society, Pipestone, Minnesota; Emmons County Historical Society, Linton, North Dakota; and Yankton County Museum, Yankton, South Dakota.

Publication of this book was made possible in part by grants from the North Dakota Humanities Council and from the Faculty Research Committee, the Office of Research and Program Development, the College of Arts and Sciences, the Office of the President, and the University of North Dakota Foundation – all at the University of North Dakota.

The second printing was made possible through the generosity of a private donor and by grants from the Professional Development Fund in the University of North Dakota History Department, the University of North Dakota Foundation, and the North Dakota State Historical Society.

Introduction

"They are a part of the history of North and South Dakota."
A South Dakota farmer

In the summer of 1979, I was a member of a Chautauqua troupe that performed on the shores of Silver Lake near the Sargent County town of Rutland, located a short distance north of the state boundary in southeastern North Dakota. During a free afternoon, an elderly but energetic gentleman from Rutland named Ole Breum took the members of the group on a tour of the area's historical sites. The route of the tour took us across the state line and through the Tewaukon National Wildlife Refuge on the Sisseton and Wahpeton Indian Reservation. It was on this tour that Breum introduced me to the quartzite monuments that were set to stand every half mile on the boundary between the states of North and South Dakota.

Ole Breum, who celebrated his eighty-fourth birthday in February 1988, represented the Rutland community for five terms in the North Dakota legislature between 1953 and 1965. While in Bismarck, Breum tried to alert his legislative colleagues to what was happening to the boundary monuments. He wanted the rocks removed that have been piled around the monuments, those righted that have fallen or are leaning from the perpendicular, those returned that have been taken, and those preserved that remain. Breum's efforts were frustrated by the press of legislative business; by the lack of interest among other legislators; and by the reality that because they stand on the boundary, the monuments involve the people, governments, and agencies of two states. Since 1979, I have come to share Breum's concern for the monuments.

Ole Breum, Rutland, North Dakota. Photo by the author.

I have always been attracted to the quartzite that is found in the vicinity of Sioux Falls, South Dakota. While I was growing up on a farm in the period before World War II, my parents frequently took my brothers and me with them when they went to Sioux Falls for shopping and business. At that time, on Main and Phillips avenues, for example, one could still find many buildings that had been constructed of Sioux Falls quartzite and some city streets still paved with quartzite blocks. I thought that quartzite was the most beautiful building stone I had ever seen. Sioux Falls quartzite still appeals to me, not only because it is pleasing to my senses of sight and touch, but also because it possesses

Washington High School, Sioux Falls, South Dakota, built of quartzite. As it looked during the author's childhood, ca. 1930s. R. E. Kolbe Dakota Collection.

Carnegie Library, Sioux Falls, South Dakota, built of quartzite, now the Civic Fine Arts Center. Much as it looked during the author's childhood. R. E. Kolbe Dakota Collection.

Children's Home, Sioux Falls, South Dakota, built of quartzite, much as it looked during the author's childhood. Razed for the Lewis Drug Eastgate Store. R. E. Kolbe Dakota Collection.

School for the Deaf, Sioux Falls, South Dakota, built of quartzite during the late 1880s. The author remembers taking school-sponsored field trips to the institution. R. E. Kolbe Dakota Collection.

character, represents solidity, and bespeaks the past.

Although I had long known that quartzite was used as a building stone, not until the beginning of my friendship with Ole Breum in 1979 did I learn that the boundary between North and South Dakota was marked with stone monuments of Sioux Falls quartzite. To say that my interest was aroused when Breum introduced me to the monuments would be an understatement. I cannot explain the attraction they had for me nor the hold they have come to have on me.

The history of North and South Dakota being neither my teaching nor research field, I tried to learn something about the boundary monuments from those whose field it was. To my surprise, I discovered that almost nothing had been written about the quartzite monuments. Indeed, many residents of both North and South Dakota did not know that the monuments existed. So began my research on the monuments and my attachment to Dakota's quartzite boundary.

My search for information led me to local, state, and national archives. Next to seeing and touching the monuments themselves, my greatest thrill was to find the original survey notes of Charles H. Bates, the United States surveyor who surveyed the boundary between North and South Dakota in 1891 and 1892 and marked it with 720 quartzite monuments. I also located Bates' correspondence with the Interior Department and the General Land Office in Washington, D.C., and learned that the boundary between the two Dakotas is the only one of its length in the nation marked with such prominent stone monuments.

I do not pretend to have any more feel for the past than do other historians, and I am keenly aware of my limitations in being able to share that feeling with others. The extent to which I can do either in regards to the boundary monuments, however, is due largely to the sense of history conveyed to me by Bates' survey notes and his correspondence.

I did research in field notes, documents, newspapers, and other sources in my office, but it was the monuments themselves in which I was most interested. To many people, any one of the monuments remaining of the original 720 must look very much like another, but to me each has its own individuality. Some have stories connected with them – many may be no more than local lore, but others must be true.

For the past eight years, I have spent a part of each summer walking along the state line, studying and photographing the monuments. Except for about fifty miles in the area of the Badlands along the Little Missouri River, I have walked the entire length of the boundary, much of it twice, and some of it three or four times.

Because I preferred to work alone, I began my day's walk shortly after dawn and continued until, by my calculations, I was half tired, whereupon I retraced my steps to my car. Like the man in the legend who wanted to see what was beyond the next

Standing on the west edge of the Sisseton and Wahpeton Indian Reservation, this half-mile monument doubles today as a fence post. The first boundary monument that the author saw. Photo by the author.

valley or behind the next hill, however, I was often drawn onward by the monuments and sometimes miscalculated both the amount of strength and the hours of daylight remaining to me. Sometimes, at the end of the day, I searched for my vehicle in the dark and collapsed into it – tired, but wonderfully calmed, as one who had been in communion with a close friend.

Farmers and ranchers living near the boundary were usually friendly, often helpful, and sometimes solicitous. Through much of the country that the boundary bisects, people travel by horse, trail bike, or four-wheel drive vehicle. A person on foot, therefore, is assumed to be lost, disoriented, or suffering from too much exposure to the sun. Many people went out of their way to inquire about my well-being (by which I think they meant the state of my mental health); to ask if I needed directions, a ride, or a drink of water; or to question me about what I was doing.

Many of these same people shared delightful stories about the monuments. A Mr. Fuhrer, who farms along Highway 83 south of Hague in Emmons County, North Dakota, informed me that monument 169 was broken off when hit by a running horse one cold winter night. The horse died. Fuhrer also told me about the enigmatic inscription that a young man chiseled on the east face of monument 170 while he was courting his girl in the summer of 1930. A rancher southeast of Ashley in McIntosh County, North Dakota, recounted to me how the members of a straw-baling crew from Nebraska mistook the boundary monuments on his ranch for gravestones. The men thought it strange that people would bury their dead on the open prairie – and at regular intervals of a half mile at that.

I enjoyed many memorable experiences while studying and photographing the monuments. My love for the prairie and the life it sustains was deepened. I startled and was startled by deer, antelope, and other forms of wildlife. Spending time alone on the prairie allowed me to learn much about myself, and the prairie inspired me to think some of my deepest thoughts. I was awed by the beauty of prairie sunsets. I was nearly overwhelmed by the expanse of the sky and the distance to the horizon. I was humbled by the realization that I was but a speck toiling across the face of a seemingly endless prairie.

Other experiences, although just as memorable, were not so introspective. One evening I drove into Pollock, South Dakota, after having that day walked from just north of the town to the Missouri River and back again. I was spent, but I wanted to verify my assumption that the monuments for that portion of the boundary west of the Missouri River had been shipped by steamboat from Pierre, South Dakota, and I had been directed to Robert Dale, proprietor of Dale's Recreation. Dale has a reputation for his knowledge of local history and for his large collection of newspaper clippings, which he keeps pasted in large books that once contained samples of wallpaper.

Yes, Dale recalled, he had a newspaper clipping recounting the arrival by steamboat of a shipment of monuments at a point near LaGrace, a river town that once lay on the east bank of the Missouri a short distance south of the state boundary. His scrapbooks were in the back room of the recreation parlor and he gave me permission to look at them. Just as I was about to step through the door into the back room, Dale shouted, "Watch out for the snakes!" I froze. I had been watching for rattlesnakes the entire day while walking across the prairie and had been on my guard lest one take me unawares, but I did not expect to find snakes inside a building with stout floors and walls.

Dale catches rattlesnakes and sells them to the Reptile Gardens in Rapid City, South Dakota. The walls of the back room of his recreation parlor were lined with cages, and more cages stood on the floor – all contained rattlesnakes. The snakes could not get at me, but I was certain that they were all trying to.

As enjoyable as my research was, it also raised disturbing and perplexing questions. Do the boundary monuments any longer serve a useful purpose? Does anyone "own" them and does this ownership entail responsibility? As the centennial of their being set approaches, what should be done, if anything, to call attention to the monuments? Will calling attention to them only make them the more vulnerable to being defaced or removed? Should the monuments be preserved? If so, why, and by whom?

In the Dakotas today, fences and roads neatly divide the land into the tiny squares shown on the township plats. Because it is unlikely that anyone will become disoriented or lost along the boundary today, the monuments are no longer of "special utility to the wayfarer," as they were in November 1891 when the Yankton *Press and Dakotan* published Bates' account of the work that he had completed during that year's surveying season.

The boundary between North and South Dakota is a thin, imaginary line that no one can "own." What about the monuments? Are they private property? Those on whose land the monuments stand or those who have taken them to adorn their lawns, grace their drives, or serve as the mantles over their fireplaces may not take kindly to being told that they do not have clear title to them. Ownership of the monuments and the responsibility for their maintenance and preservation are complex issues.

The ownership of the monuments and the responsibility of caring for them may be issues that will have to be ruled on by a state attorney general – two of them, in fact, because two states are involved. Therein lies a difficulty. The attorneys general, legislatures, historical societies, and citizens of two states would have to be mobilized and their actions coordinated. Not an easy task.

The boundary between the two Dakotas was surveyed and marked at federal expense. But it is doubtful that the federal government any longer claims title to the monuments. And it is unlikely that the federal government would assume any responsibility for maintaining and preserving them. Do the two Dakotas then own the monuments, and do they have the responsibility of caring for them?

Contrary to the opinions of those on whose land the monuments stand or of those who have removed monuments to their own property, in all likelihood they do not own them. The monuments may in fact belong to the people of North and South Dakota. But when something belongs to everybody, it belongs to nobody. People must become educated as to the existence of the monuments, to their uniqueness, and to their significance in Dakota history. Educating people and galvanizing them to action are difficult and time consuming – and drawing attention to the monuments might make them the more vulnerable to being removed or defaced.

As to their preservation, the monuments do not need so much to be preserved as to be left alone. Quartzite is durable and the monuments can fend for themselves, except those whose bases are being eroded away by the elements. Humans pose the greatest danger to the monuments, and they alone can prevent their being vandalized or moved. The rocks that have been piled around the monuments can be removed, but someone would have to take the initiative and bear the cost. The monuments that have fallen could be reset, but someone would have to do the work. And perhaps those who have "found" monuments or "purchased" them can have the better sides of their nature appealed to and be persuaded to return the monuments to their original settings. But will they allow themselves to be persuaded?

A half-mile monument nearly covered by the rocks that have been piled around it. The Coteau des Prairie near Sisseton, South Dakota, in the background. Photo by the author.

I cannot expect others to share my attachment to the monuments. Let us not, however, dismiss them as having outlasted their usefulness. A South Dakota farmer living near Hankinson, North Dakota, confessed to me that the monuments are a nuisance to farm around. But, he added, "I wouldn't dream of destroying or removing one of them. They are a part of the history of North and South Dakota."

Indeed they are. Even if we have not seen or touched one of the monuments, yes, even if we have not so much as heard of them, they are a part of each one of us by virtue of their being woven into the warp and woof of our history.

With President Benjamin Harrison, who with a pen fashioned from an eagle's quill created the twin states of North and South Dakota where there had been but one territory; with South Dakota Senator Richard F. Pettigrew, who had an abiding faith in the properties of quartzite and in the future of the Sioux Falls stone industry; with Charles H. Bates, who alone of United States surveyors marked a state boundary of such a length with impressive monoliths; with the men of Bates' survey party, who endured death-dealing blizzards, searing heat, and ravenous mosquitoes to set the monuments and who must at times have cursed their bulk and weight; and with surveyor George G. Beardsley, who testified that the monuments were "uniform and nicely set"—we are all inextricably linked to the monuments. They are a part of our past and—I hope—our future.

Chapter 1

From Territory to States

"They were born together – they were one and I will make them twins."
President Benjamin Harrison

Like silent sentinels, hundreds of magnificent quartzite monuments have faithfully guarded the border between the states of North Dakota and South Dakota for almost one hundred years. Placed every half mile along the boundary by United States surveyor Charles H. Bates and his surveying party, the monuments are not mentioned in any of the many histories written of the two states, nor are they known to most residents of the states. The monuments, among the states' treasures, make their common boundary unique. No other state boundary of comparable length in the nation is marked along its entire length with such impressive monuments. Described by United States surveyor George G. Beardsley, who examined Bates' work, as a "marvel of accuracy" and by the Steele *Ozone* as "the most perfect and comprehensive boundary line in the United States," the boundary between North and South Dakota was established on the seventh standard parallel and was surveyed and marked by Bates during the surveying seasons of 1891 and 1892.

Before becoming states, North Dakota and South Dakota had been almost equal parts of Dakota Territory, an entity created by an act of Congress in 1861. As provided by the Northwest Ordinance of 1787, the inhabitants of a territory, when their numbers had reached 60,000, could write a constitution, form a state government, and apply for statehood. Until such time, the President of the United States appointed the governor and other territorial officers, and the people of the territory elected their own representatives to the territorial legislature. The inhabitants of the territory also sent a nonvoting delegate to the United States House of Representatives. Because the Northwest Ordinance defined the procedure by which statehood could be attained, territorial status was clearly intended to be temporary, a period of tutelage until such time as the inhabitants were deemed capable of assuming the responsibilities attendant upon statehood.

For most territories the period of tutelage was short. In the case of Minnesota Territory, for example, the period lasted only from 1849 to 1858. The region organized as Dakota Territory in 1861, however, endured territorial status until 1889, and during this twenty-eight year period a protracted struggle ensued between those who sought statehood and those who tried to delay or prevent it.

The drive for statehood was evident very early in Dakota – petitions advocating division of the territory into two states appeared in Congress as early as 1870. The discussions taking place all over the territory at that time culminated in the territorial legislature's adopting a memorial on January 12, 1871, asking the United States Congress to divide the territory into two parts, the division to be made on the forty-sixth parallel of north latitude. Almost every year thereafter, the territorial legislature transmitted to Congress a petition from some organization asking that two states be formed from the territory and admitted into the Union on an equal footing with the existing states. The territorial legislature itself adopted resolutions on December 31, 1872; December 19, 1874; and January 24, 1877 – all containing the same request.

Although there was strong sentiment for dividing the territory into two states, other alternatives were proposed. On January 7, 1880, Granville G. Bennett, the territorial delegate to Congress, presented a bill to the House of Representatives providing for admission into the Union of all that part of Dakota south of the forty-sixth parallel as a state and the formation of the balance into a territory to be called Pembina. Other bills were introduced authorizing the admission of Dakota as a state, without division. On December 19, 1881, Richard F. Pettigrew, then territorial delegate to Congress, introduced two bills; one provided for the admission of all that part of the territory south of the forty-sixth parallel into the Union as a state, and the other called for the organization of the north half of the territory into the territory of North Dakota.

Another proposal was that the territory be divided into two states, but east and west of a line drawn down the middle of the territory rather than north and south of the forty-sixth parallel. Yet another called for the division of the territory into three states.

The statehood movement began in earnest during the 1880s and, because of circumstances, assumed the characteristics of a revolt of the territory's inhabitants against outside interests. Farmers, organized into the Dakota Farmers' Alliance, revolted against the outside exploitation by the railroads, the banks, the grain traders, and the machinery manufacturers. Farmers sought economic equality of status in the nation; and the inhabitants of the territory sought political equality of status in the nation.

There was also an internal revolt of sorts, engendered by the bitterness and suspicion between the northern and southern parts of the territory. The southern portion of Dakota Territory was more developed and enjoyed a much larger population than the northern portion (in 1890 South Dakota had 328,808 inhabitants, but North Dakota had only 182,719). In 1877 "South" Dakota had twenty-nine of the thirty-six seats in the territorial legislature and controlled not only the territorial legislature, but also the territorial delegate to Congress. The territorial capital was in the south, at Yankton, and the "Yankton oligarchy" virtually controlled territorial affairs.

Yankton in 1880. The capital of Dakota Territory until 1883, when it was moved to Bismarck. South Dakota State Historical Society.

Inhabitants of the northern portion of the territory also shared the fear, not ungrounded, that South Dakota would be admitted into the Union as a state while the northern portion would continue to be exploited as a territory. Even the choice of names evoked suspicion. "Lincoln" and "Pembina" were suggested as names for the northern part of the territory, and to members of Congress and to most people in the nation the matter of naming was inconsequential. But during territorial days, "Dakota No. 1 Hardwheat," or "Dakota Red," had been so extensively advertised that no one living in the northern half of the territory could accept a name that omitted the word "Dakota."

Statehood for the two Dakotas was indeed accomplished by revolution, but as Elwyn B. Robinson noted in his *History of North Dakota,* it was "a quiet revolution," one accomplished by fewer than two hundred men. Howard R. Lamar in his book

The Reverend Joseph Ward, reform-minded promoter of statehood for the Dakotas. J. L. Jennewein and Jane Boorman, eds., Dakota Panorama.

Dakota Territory, 1861-1889 agrees with Robinson's figure of two hundred, but noted that of this number only a dozen were politically prominent. Some were honest men and true reformers, such as General William Henry Harrison Beadle, the Reverend Joseph Ward, and Father Robert Haire. Most of the leaders, however, were singularly unimpressed and untouched by radical political ideas or social reform programs (although South Dakota's motto "Under God The People Rule" pays lip service to the early reform sentiment).

The movement for statehood may have appeared to some as a broad, many-faceted movement, but it was not. Statehood became a reality through the efforts of a few men who knew how to move people and manipulate party machinery. They feared all radical reforms and were frightened by the rural voters' increasing interest in politics. They were determined that the only change to be accomplished by statehood was the substitution of local for federal control of patronage. In time, many farmers came to realize that the leaders of the statehood movement were the same kind of men who ran the territorial government, who held the mortgages on their farms, who sold them their farm machinery and supplies, and who bought their wheat at ruinously low prices.

Lamar refined his figure of a dozen men even further and asserted that five men and their personal following secured statehood for North and South Dakota and offices for themselves: Hugh J. Campbell, Gideon C. Moody, Arthur C. Mellette, Alonzo Edgerton, and Richard F. Pettigrew. Only Campbell failed to secure high office. Pettigrew and Moody became South Dakota's first senators, Mellette became the state's first governor, and Edgerton became judge of the United States circuit court for South Dakota. Pettigrew, a skilled politician and party manager, was the Republican boss of the Big Sioux River Valley. Trained as a land surveyor and as a lawyer, he was an enthusiastic boomer of Sioux Falls and owned what was perhaps South Dakota's largest real estate business.

Richard F. Pettigrew in 1895, surveyor, lawyer, promoter, and politician. Siouxland Heritage Museums, Sioux Falls, South Dakota.

Arthur C. Mellette, last governor of Dakota Territory and first governor of South Dakota. J. L. Jennewein and Jane Boorman, eds., Dakota Panorama.

The two hundred men to whom Robinson and Lamar referred formed the "Yankton oligarchy." They were the professional politicians and the business and professional men in the southern portion of the territory. They considered themselves to be (and they were) members of a distinct social, economic, and political class. A majority were from New England, New York, and the Old Northwest.

Being bankers, lawyers, and editors, they shared middle-class beliefs and were ethnically Old American and Protestant. They were almost without exception Republicans, because Dakota was a one-party region, a result of the long years of territorial status during which the Republican party controlled the United States government. Many were members of the Grand Army of the Republic and all were keenly interested in politics. They were in the territorial assembly; they held county offices; they controlled the territorial delegation to Washington; and they dominated territorial Republican conventions.

These men wrote the South Dakota constitutions of 1883, 1885, and 1889. It is a tribute to their abilities that, although the territory's population increased from 135,000 in 1880 to more than 500,000 in 1890, they retained economic and political control and were able to control large numbers of German and Scandinavian voters and prevent them for winning any major office.

These men were tired of the president's appointing the governor and territorial officials from outside the territory. They wanted elective offices for themselves. Their sentiments were expressed in the Yankton *Press and Dakotaian,* the territory's most prominent newspaper, in 1877:

> We are so heartily disgusted with our dependent condition, with being snubbed at every turn in life, with having all our interests subjected to the whims and corrupt acts of persons in power that we feel very much as the thirteen colonies felt when they flung away their dependent condition and asserted their position among nations.

Oscar S. Gifford from Canton, located south of Sioux Falls on the Big Sioux River, laced his disgust with bitterness. Gifford had been the town's mayor, he owned considerable real estate, he was a stalwart Republican, and he was an earnest advocate of dividing Dakota Territory into two states at the forty-sixth parallel. In February 1888 Gifford appeared before the Committee on Territories of the United States House of Representatives to plead the cause for statehood. He reminded committee members that the population, resources, and institutions of Dakota entitled the people to statehood. Then, in words that deserve a place in the annals of Dakota, he indicted the territorial system under which Dakota languished. "Dakota today," he said,

Oscar S. Gifford, South Dakota's first representative to Congress. Clement A. Lounsberry, North Dakota, History and People.

> is a territory only in name. In every condition and as a fact, it is a mere colony or province, as completely was ever attached to the British Empire, a condition of affairs never intended or contemplated by the founders of this government, and is most repugnant to the spirit of our institutions. The government which is provided for the territories of the United States is almost identical with that which was extended by England over her colonies a century and a half ago, and against which the fathers of this republic so successfully rebelled.

Reformers, such as General William Henry Harrison Beadle, territorial superintendent of public instruction, promoted the campaign for statehood in its initial stages. In order to safeguard school lands (sections 16 and 36 in each township) and prevent their being sold or rented for less than their value, Beadle supported a campaign to form a separate state from the southern part of the territory. The territorial administration was unable to utilize or conserve the resources represented by the school lands (the school sections constituted one-eighteenth of the land in the territory and totalled over five million acres). Squatters were occupying and cultivating thousands of acres – exhausting the soil and

William Henry Harrison Beadle, territorial superintendent of public instruction and promoter of statehood for the Dakotas. George W. Kingsbury, History of Dakota Territory.

paying nothing for its use. There was no territorial authority to take possession of the school lands, and the legal steps taken to prevent trespassing were not generally effective. Beadle wanted constitutional restrictions on the sale of school land and the establishment of a minimum price of ten dollars per acre, the proceeds to be set aside for education.

Beadle and his friends furthered the cause for statehood through statehood clubs and in private discussions. A Citizen's Constitutional Association, sponsored by Beadle, Ward, and others, called for a convention to meet at Canton on June 21, 1882. An important accomplishment of this convention was the formation of the Dakota Citizens' League, which continued to work for statehood and reform. Reflecting the reform mindedness of the convention was the work of the Committee on Resolutions, headed by Ward. The committee provided for the protection of the future school fund with the provision that school lands should not be sold for less than ten dollars per acre. Receipts from sales were to be placed in a perpetual fund for the support of schools. Beadle's "Dakota plan," as it was called, was inserted in the Omnibus Bill authorizing statehood in 1889 and in the constitutions of all four states admitted to the Union that year – North Dakota, South Dakota, Montana, and Washington.

In 1883 a bill was introduced in Congress that provided for statehood for the southern counties of Dakota and the continuation of territorial status for the northern counties. It did not pass. Subsequently, another convention assembled in Sioux Falls on September 8, 1885, to draft a constitution – essentially the 1883 document slightly revised – and frame a government. Although a slate of officials was selected and Huron designated as the capital, Washington again frustrated the cause for statehood.

Another impetus for statehood was disgust with the corruption in the office of Nehemiah G. Ordway, the territorial governor who was, if it came to that, a single-state man. Before becoming governor of Dakota, Ordway had been a member of the New Hampshire senate and had secured his appointment through the influence of New Hampshire businessmen with investments in Dakota. Ordway built a powerful political machine by securing appointments for people he had brought with him when he came to the territory and by enlisting the support of influential newspaper editors

Nehemiah G. Ordway, governor of Dakota Territory, removed in 1884. South Dakota State Historical Society.

through his control of advertising sales of public land.

Ordway forged an alliance with Alexander McKenzie, who was the political agent in northern Dakota for the Northern Pacific Railroad, the representative of powerful financial interests in Minneapolis and St. Paul, and the political boss of what was to become North Dakota. This alliance made possible in 1883 the removal of the territorial capital from Yankton to Bismarck, to which the Northern Pacific had built in 1873 before suspending work due to the economic depression of that year.

Yankton's location in the southeastern corner of the huge territory (Dakota contained 96,596,480 acres and was larger than any state or territory in the Union, except Texas and California) made it an unattractive site for the territorial capital. The primary reason for removing the capital, however, was the Northern Pacific's desire

Capital of Dakota Territory, Bismarck. J. L. Jennewein and Jane Boorman, eds., Dakota Panorama.

to have the capital on its main line at Bismarck, beyond which construction had begun again in 1879. The Northern Pacific had vital interests in the northern portion of the territory – and a powerful influence in the same proportion – because of the large land grant it had received from the federal government. The land grant amounted to 10,700,000 acres, twenty-four percent of the area that later comprised North Dakota.

The Yankton group resented the removal of the capital from Yankton to Bismarck. They also circulated accounts of Governor Ordway's corrupt dealings. Charges ranged from his withholding patronage and refusing to sign bills until his son's appointment as territorial auditor was confirmed to offering county commissioner positions for sale to the highest bidder and accepting $30,000 in cash for his part in removing the capital from Yankton to Bismarck.

President Chester A. Arthur removed Ordway as territorial governor in June 1884. By making it appear with their charges that the territorial government was hopelessly corrupt, the Yankton group had significantly advanced the cause of statehood.

The dislike of outside control clothed naked motivations of self-interest with the respectable demand for "home rule," but there was very little popular interest in Dakota for statehood. Farmers were too preoccupied with crops and prices and miners were too interested in digging for gold to be bothered with constitutional issues. Nor were the Dakota Democrats and such men as Ordway, McKenzie, and their supporters enthusiastic about the prospect of statehood.

After 1883 and the removal of the territorial capital from Yankton to Bismarck, there was a contest between the factions who, for selfish reasons, believed that the territory was ready for and entitled to self-government and those who, for equally selfish reasons, wanted the territory to remain a ward of the United States government. McKenzie and other Bismarck leaders opposed statehood because they preferred to have Bismarck remain the capital of a large territory.

Powerful outside interests such as the railroads also opposed statehood for Dakota. They preferred the lenient territorial railroad laws, and through their influence in Washington, they could influence or control territorial appointments. Absentee railroad companies owned every main line in Dakota Territory, and not one of the directors or high officials of any of the major lines running through the territory was a Dakotan. Political policy for the territory was often made by the managers of the Northern Pacific; the Chicago, Milwaukee & St. Paul; and the Chicago & North Western Railway companies. According to Howard R. Lamar, the last five territorial governors of Dakota were all men picked and approved by these three railway companies. After his removal as territorial governor in 1884, Ordway was retained by the Northern Pacific as lobbyist in Washington to oppose statehood for Dakota.

Financial interests also opposed statehood for Dakota. Between 1880-1890 Dakota Territory attracted millions of dollars in eastern and foreign investments at interest rates ranging up to twenty percent. With its bonanza farms, with its burgeoning sheep and cattle industries, with its land and mineral resources, and with its demand for farm machinery and supplies, Dakota Territory was an investor's paradise.

In his remarks to the Committee on Territories of the United States House of Representatives in early February 1888, Oscar S. Gifford noted that Dakota Territory in 1887 had 62 national banks and 237 private banks. George W. Kingsbury noted in his *History of Dakota Territory* that there were more banks in Dakota Territory than there were in the eight states of North Carolina, West Virginia, Florida, Mississippi, Louisiana, Arkansas, Delaware, and Nevada combined. Eastern financiers and investors wanted to prevent statehood for Dakota as a means of avoiding state control of loans and interest rates.

And there were outside political obstacles to statehood. Members of Congress believed the population of Dakota Territory insufficient to justify the formation of two states, and most of those supporting statehood strongly resisted any suggestion that Dakota be a single state. The more populous states were also jealous of their influence in the United States Senate and did not relish the prospect of admitting the thinly settled area of Dakota to an equal voice with themselves in this relatively exclusive political club.

Members of Congress before 1888 also readily perceived that among the supporters of statehood the desire for self-rule and professions of disinterestedness masked motivations of self-interest. The tone of congressional debates reflected the well-founded suspicion that political jobbers in Dakota were more interested in retaining the capital at Yankton, curbing the political influence of the Northern Pacific, and controlling patronage than they were in achieving self-government for the people of Dakota. The Democratic editor of the Yankton *Dakota Herald* on February 26, 1881, described the members of the territorial legislature as "a howling mob of gangsters and corruptionists, caring nothing for right or law, but led by the nose by one or two tricksters whose whole object was to fill their pockets by schemes of jobbery and plunder."

Senators and congressmen who enjoyed the benefits and advantages accruing to them through their control of the patronage of a territory also did not want to surrender the power of appointment to one or two new states. The Democrats, except for short periods, also controlled at least one house of the Congress during the 1880s, and the Democratic party wanted to prevent the admission of any state that would send Republican senators and representatives to Washington and add Republican votes to the electoral college.

Moreover, wrote William B. Henessey in his *History of North Dakota,* Congress paid little heed – for obvious reasons – to the many petitions sent after 1871 asking that the territory of Dakota be divided and admitted into the Union as two states. In the East, Dakota was regarded as a savage wilderness; to do anything that would encourage people to settle in the territory was viewed as being tantamount to the commission of a crime. The territory was also governed by carpetbaggers who were selected for their political activity elsewhere and who had nothing in common with the people of the territory. It was not in human nature that they would legislate their jobs out of existence.

After the Democratic victory in 1884 that brought Grover Cleveland into the White House and gave the Democrats control of Congress for the first time in over twenty years, the prospect for statehood appeared to be bleak. The administration knew that statehood for Dakota would mean at least two more Republican senators in Washington. If two states were formed from Dakota, there was the possibility of four more Republican senators.

Shortly after his election, President Cleveland appointed Louis Kossuth Church as governor and Michael L. McCormack as secretary of the territory. Church was a New York lawyer and a friend of James J. Hill, the future "empire builder" who became the key figure in the railroads of North Dakota. McCormack was a member of the Bismarck group who opposed statehood. Both Church and McCormack opposed statehood because the Democrats wanted to control territorial patronage, and party leaders believed that with a few years of Democratic control the northern portion of Dakota might enter the Union as a Democratic state.

Louis Kossuth Church, second to last governor of Dakota Territory. J. L. Jennewein and Jane Boorman, eds., Dakota Panorama.

The removal of the territorial capital from Yankton to Bismarck led to a redoubling of the efforts on the part of the southern counties for separate statehood and also to an acceptance of statehood rather than continued territorial status for the northern counties. Nor was there any longer the steadfast resistance to sharing with the northern counties the distinctive name "Dakota." There had been, wrote Henessey in his *History of North Dakota,* a change of attitude:

> In the days when there were not enough people in the entire territory to get up a decent political row – and that was long ago – there was a disposition on the part of those whites who had settled in the southeastern part of Dakota to procure a political divorce from the northern portion of the vast territory. The southern Dakotans had but a contemptuous disregard for the country of the half-breeds and, though they themselves had little to be proud of, they were impressed with the idea that they would get along better if separated from that part of the territory lying along the international boundary. And the few people living in what is now North Dakota had no particular objection to the granting of the divorce.

In the presidential campaign of 1888, the Republican party made the admission into the Union of the two states of Dakota a plank in its platform. The bill providing for southern Dakota's becoming a state and northern Dakota's remaining a territory had been dropped in favor of a bill providing for the admission of two states. Senator Benjamin Harrison of Indiana, the Republican presidential candidate, strongly supported the bill. Moreover, the large population of Dakota made further denial of statehood seem unjust and irresponsible.

Statehood for the two Dakotas also came closer to being a reality when Ordway and both the Dakota and national Democrats dropped their single-state bill. The Republican successes in the election of 1888 had made the Democrats more conciliatory. If an enabling act were passed during the lame duck session of 1888-1889, wrote Herbert S. Schell in his *History of South Dakota,* the Democrats could claim credit for it and expect to reap political advantages from it.

The continuation of territorial tuteluge was also seen as a dangerous usurpation of government by Congress, and it posed the danger that it might lead to the national government's dictating in state and local government. Moreover, Dakota Territory was expensive for the federal government to maintain. Only about ten percent of the costs of administering the territory was raised from territorial and local taxes; the remainder came from the national treasury. National control of the territorial system was seen as being small compensation for the costs involved in administering the territory.

Both Republicans and Democrats voted for the Omnibus Bill that authorized the framing of constitutions in North Dakota, South Dakota, Montana, and Washington. President Cleveland appropriately celebrated Washington's birthday by signing the bill on February 22, 1889, at 11:00 a.m. Passage of the Omnibus Bill meant that four new states would enter the Union during the centennial of George Washington's inaugural as the first president of the newly created United States of America.

The territorial government of Dakota ceased to exist on November 2, 1889, when President Benjamin Harrison signed the proclamations admitting North and South Dakota into the Union. There had been some rivalry between the two states for the honor of being the first to be admitted to the Union, but President Harrison declined to settle the issue by making a choice. He had Secretary of State James G. Blaine shuffle the papers and cover them so he could not tell which proclamation he signed first. The signing took place at 3:40 p.m. on

November 2, 1889. Both North and South Dakota were born into the sisterhood of states within the same moment. To sign the proclamations, Harrison used a pen fashioned from the quill of an eagle that had been shot in the northern part of the territory.

The formal proclamation was unique in that it gave, at the same instant, legal status as sovereign states to two autonomous bodies – North Dakota and South Dakota. When notifying Governors John Miller and Arthur C. Mellette in Bismarck of the president's action, Blaine wrote:

> The last act in the admission of the two Dakotas as states in the Union was completed this afternoon at the executive mansion at three o'clock and forty minutes by the President signing at that moment the proclamation required by law for the admission of the two states.
>
> . . . This is the first instance in the history of the national government of twin states. North and South Dakota entered the Union at the same moment.

South Dakota had a valid claim to being the older of the two states because it was the first to form a state legislature and elect senators. South Dakota's officials were inaugurated on Saturday, November 2, the day the proclamation was signed; North Dakota's officers were not inaugurated until Monday, November 4. South Dakota's government was, therefore, in lawful operation two days before that of North Dakota.

South Dakota's claim to being the older state notwithstanding (by common agreement arrived at later, North Dakota holds thirty-ninth and South Dakota fortieth rank among the states of the Union), Blaine's message to the governors of the two new states provides the evidence that both came into the Union at the same moment. President Harrison did not want to know which proclamation he signed first, and, according to Blaine, the President remarked, "They were born together – they were one and I will make them twins."

Chapter 2

Establishing the Boundary

"The territory of Dakota shall . . . be divided on the line of the seventh standard parallel. . . . "
Omnibus Bill

With the stroke of a pen (or of a quill, to be more precise), President Benjamin Harrison created North and South Dakota. Creating sovereign states from a previously existing territory entails more, however, than affixing a signature to a proclamation. Capitals had to be established – in Pierre and Bismarck ("two of the loneliest landscapes on the continent," wrote John Milton in his *South Dakota, A Bicentennial History*). Constitutions had to be written, legislatures elected, and officials chosen. Legislative and judicial districts had to be reapportioned. Between the two new states, an equitable division had to be made not only of the former territory's debts, but also of its assets, including territorial documents, the books in the territorial library, and the arms and rounds of ammunition in the territorial armory.

The South Dakota constitutional convention met at Sioux Falls in September 1889, and on October 1, 1889, the voters ratified the constitution and elected Arthur C. Mellette as their first governor. The seventy-five members of the North Dakota constitutional convention met in Bismarck on July 4, 1889. Included in the festivities marking the event was a big parade, with several hundred Sioux from the Standing Rock Reservation taking part. They were led by Sitting Bull who carried a large American flag. On August 17 the convention concluded its forty-five-day session. On October 1, 1889, North Dakota voters approved the constitution by a vote of 27,441 to 8,107. John Miller was elected as the state's first governor.

Henry C. Hansbrough, North Dakota's first representative to Congress. North Dakota Compendium of History and Biography.

The first South Dakota legislature elected Richard F. Pettigrew of Sioux Falls and Gideon C. Moody of Deadwood to be the state's first senators. North Dakota's first legislative assembly elected Gilbert Pierce and Lyman R. Casey to the United States Senate. Henry C. Hansbrough (the only person whose ashes have been scattered on Capitol Hill in Washington, D.C.), a Devils Lake newspaper editor, was sent from North Dakota to the United States House of Representatives. South Dakota's first representative was Oscar S. Gifford, who had served as territorial delegate to the Forty-ninth and Fiftieth Congresses.

As prescribed in the Enabling Act, the constitutional conventions of both North and South Dakota named a Joint Commission composed of seven members from each state whose duty it was to "agree upon an equitable division of all property belonging to the Territory of Dakota," to dispose of all public records, and also to "agree upon the amount of the debts and liabilities of

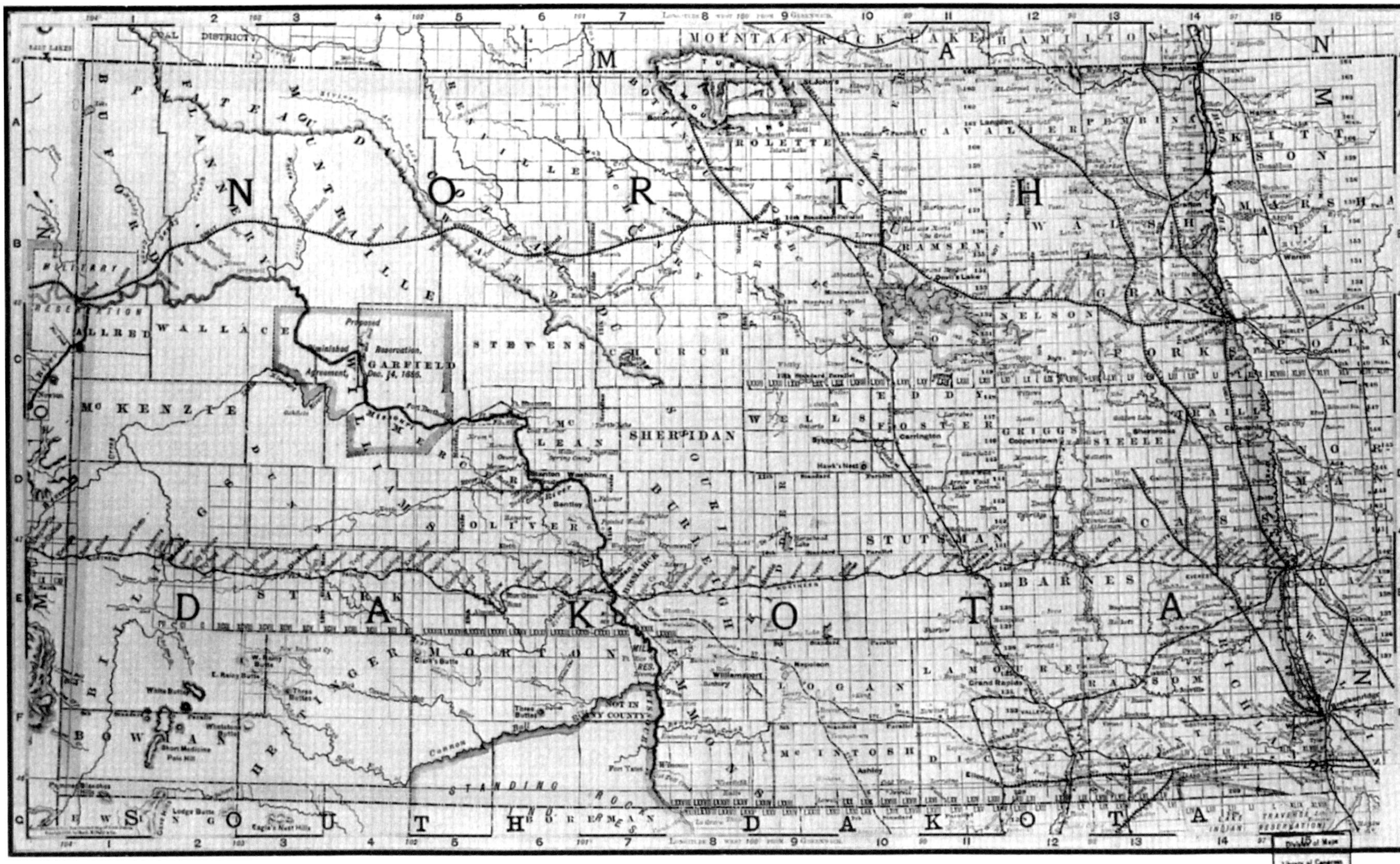

North Dakota in 1889. The forty-sixth parallel of north latitude and the approximate seventh standard parallel are shown. Both were considered for the boundary between the Dakotas. Rand, McNally and Company's New Family Atlas Map of North Dakota.

the territory which shall be assumed and paid by each of the proposed states of North Dakota and South Dakota. . . . "

Further, a boundary had to be located and drawn between the two states. Although it had long been assumed and almost universally accepted that the division of Dakota Territory would be along the forty-sixth parallel of north latitude, the Omnibus Bill, which was the Enabling Act for the Dakotas, Montana, and Washington, prescribed that the Territory of Dakota should be "divided on the line of the seventh standard parallel projected due west to the western boundary of said territory." This was the boundary provided for by the constitutional conventions of the newly formed states of North and South Dakota.

The North Dakota constitutional convention described the state's boundaries as follows:

> The State of North Dakota shall consist of all the territory included within the following boundaries, to wit: Commencing at a point in the main channel of the Red River of the North, where the forty-ninth degree of north latitude crosses the same, from thence south up the main channel of the same and along the boundary line of the State of Minnesota to a point where the seventh standard parallel intersects the same; thence west along said seventh standard parallel to a point where it intersects the twenty-seventh meridian of longitude west from Washington; then north on said meridian to a point where it intersects the forty-ninth degree of north latitude; thence east along said line to place of beginning.

The South Dakota constitutional convention described that state's borders this way:

> The boundaries of the State of South Dakota shall be as follows: Beginning at the point of intersection of the western boundary line of the State of Minnesota with the northern boundary of the State of Iowa, and running thence northerly along the western boundary line of the State of Minnesota, to its intersection with the Seventh Standard Parallel; thence west on the line of the Seventh Standard Parallel produced due west to its intersection with the Twenty-seventh Meridian of longitude west from Washington; thence south on the Twenty-seventh Meridian of longitude west from Washington to its intersection with the northern boundary line of the State of Nebraska; thence easterly along the northern boundary line of the State of Nebraska to its intersection with the western boundary line of the State of Iowa; thence northerly along the western boundary line of the State of Iowa to its intersection with the northern boundary line of the State of Iowa; thence east along the northern boundary line of the State of Iowa to the place of beginning.

Common to the descriptions of the boundaries of both North and South Dakota was the reference to the seventh standard parallel. But what was the seventh standard parallel and where was it? How was it to be located on the trackless Dakota prairie? What were the advantages of accepting the seventh standard parallel over the forty-sixth parallel as the boundary? If one parallel were used rather than the other, would states, counties, townships, farmers, and ranchers stand to gain—or lose—territory? What if the boundary should pass through federal jurisdictions such as Indian reservations, judicial districts, land office districts, and postal districts? Who would undertake the survey and, more importantly, who would pay for it? Once the boundary was surveyed, would it be marked, and, if so, how?

That these questions were matters of urgency and significance is attested to by the appointment of a Boundary Commission, consisting of members from both North and South Dakota. The South Dakota constitutional convention provided for the appointment of three commissioners to work with a similar commission from North Dakota "to supervise the Surveying, Ascertaining and Distinctly Marking the Boundary Line Between the States of North Dakota and South Dakota." The appointment of this Boundary Commission, notwithstanding, the questions involving the boundary between the two states afforded opportunity for extensive debate in both state and federal legislatures; opportunity for hard feelings between those who stood to gain or lose land, contracts, and influence; and opportunity for resourceful politicians, such as Richard F. Pettigrew, to advance their political, if not their economic, fortunes.

The forty-sixth parallel of north latitude is another of the imaginary but necessary

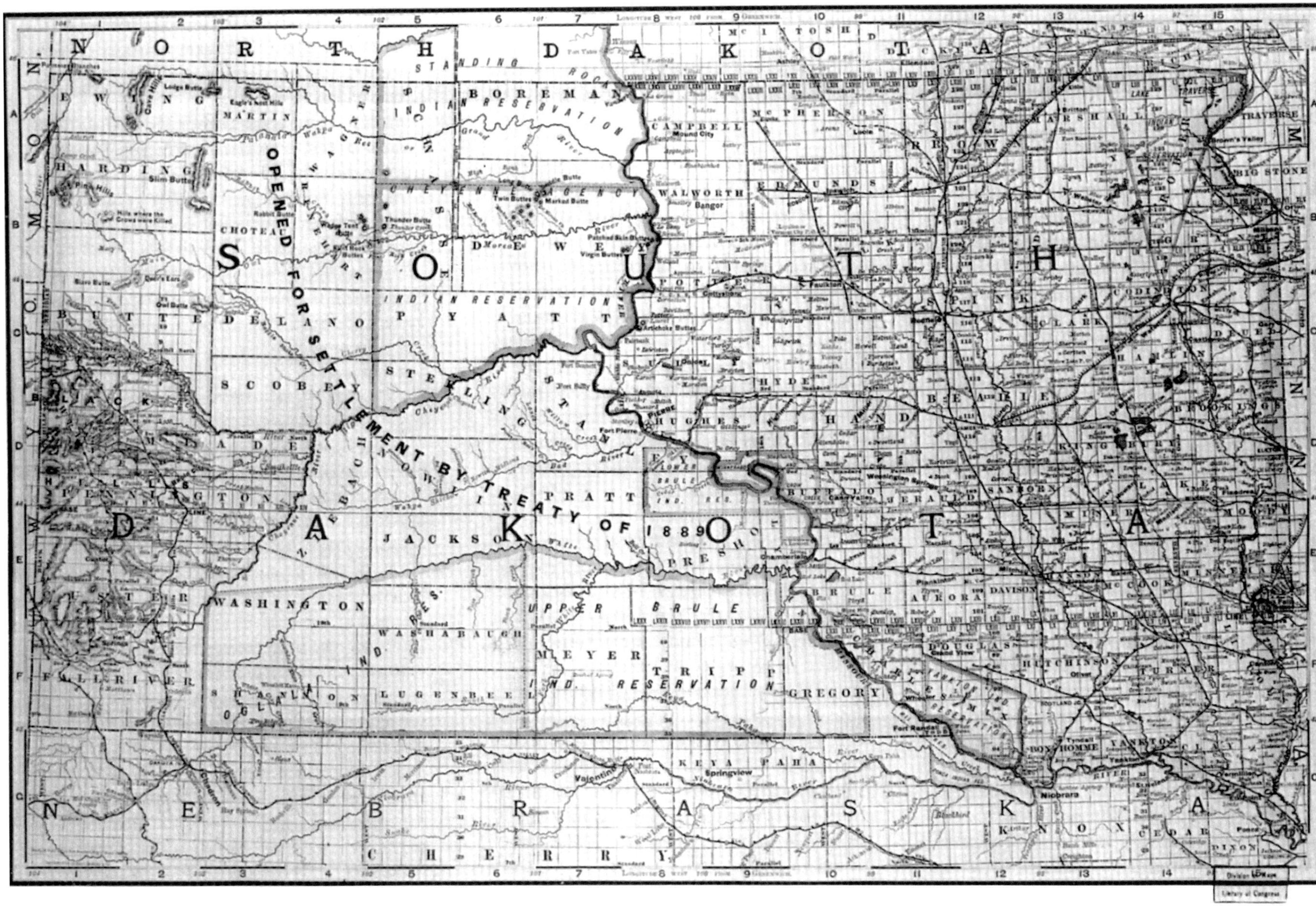

South Dakota in 1889. The wedge-shaped Sisseton and Wahpeton Indian Reservation is shown at the upper right, projecting across the state boundary. Rand, McNally and Company's New Family Atlas Map of South Dakota.

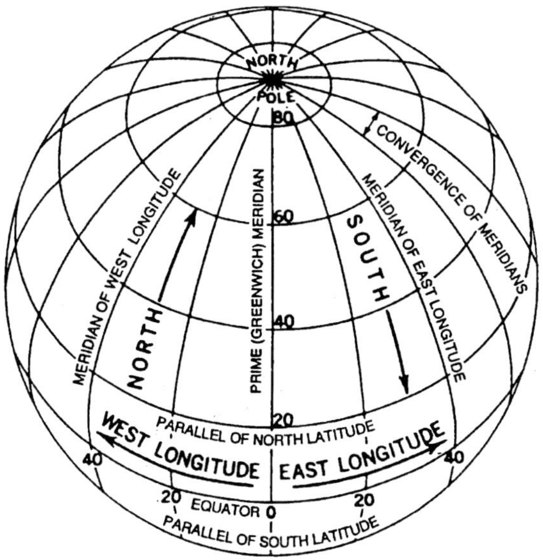

Line drawing depicting meridians of longitude and parallels of latitude. Academic Media, Graphics Department, University of North Dakota.

lines by which distances are measured and locations determined on the face of the earth. Parallels such as the forty-sixth are imaginary circles on the surface of the earth paralleling the equator and marking the latitude. The latitude of a point on the earth's surface is its angular distance from the equator, measured on the curved surface of the earth. Because a direct measurement of this distance on the surface of the earth is impracticable, it has to be determined by astronomical observations.

The western boundary of both North and South Dakota was described by the states' constitutional conventions as being the twenty-seventh meridian of longitude west from Washington, D.C. Meridians are great imaginary circles on the surface of the earth passing through the poles and any given place and numbered according to the

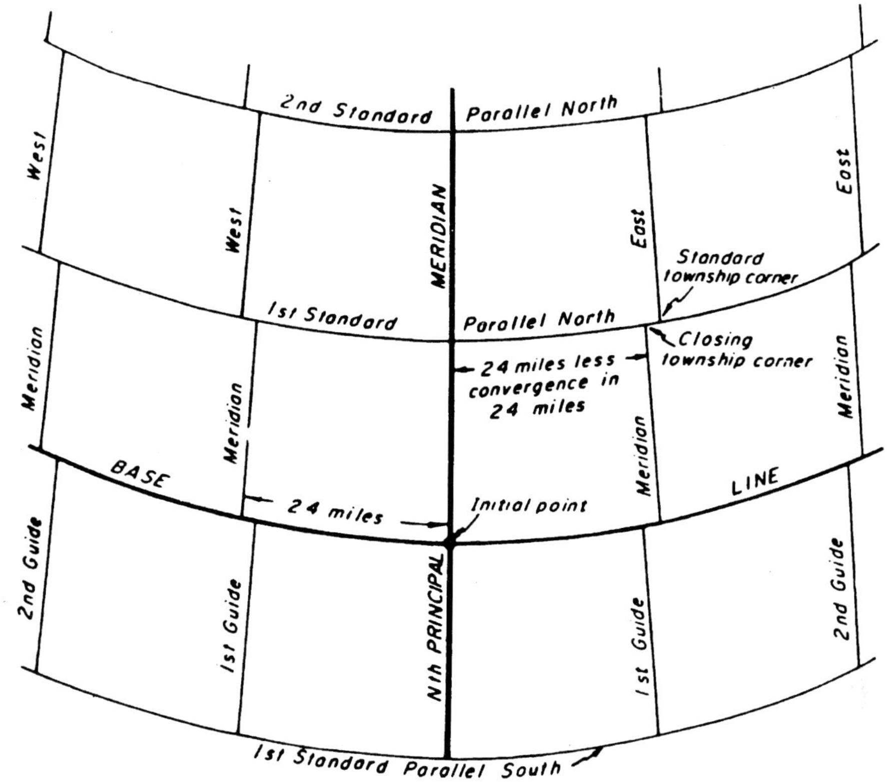

Subdivision into 24-mile tracts.

Illustration depicting standard parallels and guide meridians. Legault/McMaster/Marlett, Surveying: An Introduction to Engineering Measurements, *© 1956, p. 187. Reprinted by permission of Prentice-Hall, Inc., Englewood Cliffs, NJ.*

degrees of longitude. Because the prime meridian, from which terrestrial longitudes are reckoned, is an arbitrary line, it can be placed anywhere. For English-speaking peoples, the prime meridian has been placed so that it follows the meridian on which the Royal Observatory is located in Greenwich, England, near London. The distance between meridians is not so precise as that between parallels, because meridians converge at both of the poles.

Standard parallels, such as the seventh, are different from lines of latitude, which are also known as parallels. Standard parallels and guide meridians, which are in turn different from lines of longitude, are imaginary lines established by surveyors. Standard parallels were established at every fourth township line; guide meridians were placed at every fourth range line. These standard parallels and guide meridians form grid cells approximately twenty-four miles square, containing sixteen idealized townships.

The boundary line dividing Dakota Territory into two states was set at the forty-

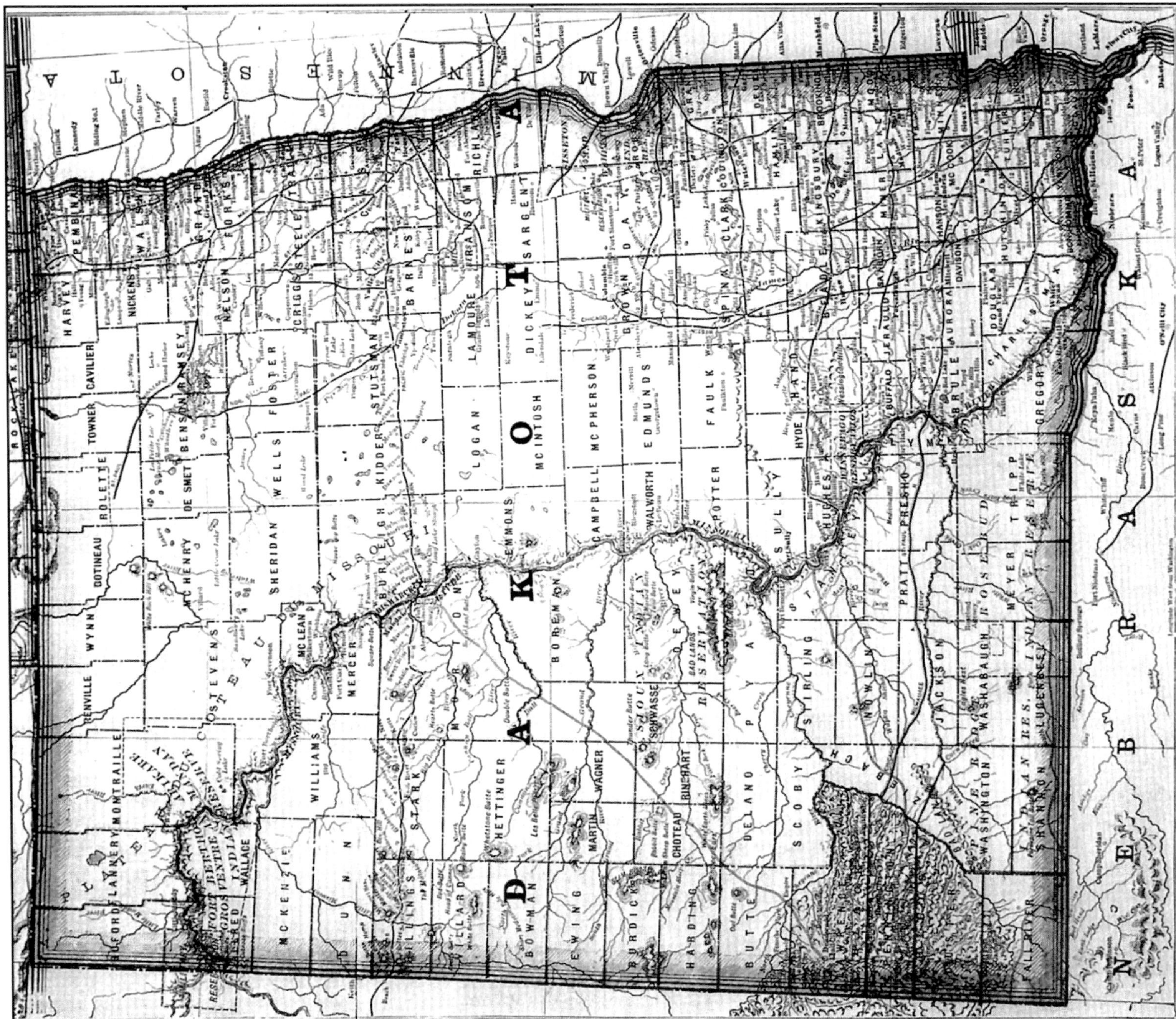

Dakota Territory. The dark lines forming the base of Emmons, McIntosh, Dickey, and Sargent counties represents approximately the seventh standard parallel. Note, however, that the line is not continuous, either west of the Missouri River or across and east of the Sisseton and Wahpeton Indian Reservation. George F. Cram. Dakota.

sixth parallel of north latitude in a bill introduced in 1880 in the United States House of Representatives by Granville G. Bennett, the territorial delegate to Congress. Bennett's bill, if passed, would also have allowed the people of Dakota to write constitutions and elect state governments.

Northern Dakota people attending a public meeting in Fargo on December 5, 1880, objected to making the forty-sixth parallel the boundary between the two states. A division along this line would have placed five-sixths of the lower tier of townships in Emmons, Logan, LaMoure, Ransom, and Richland counties on the South Dakota side of the boundary, resulting in a loss to North Dakota of large amounts of land. Not only would locating the boundary on the forty-sixth parallel have required a considerable redefining of county boundaries, in some cases it would also have resulted in homestead claims and improved farms being divided by the state boundary.

To avoid the confusion and perplexity resulting from a division of the territory along the line of the forty-sixth parallel, the Fargo convention resolved in favor of dividing the territory along the line of the seventh standard parallel. Such a line would conform to the county boundaries already established and to the township lines already drawn by congressional survey. The change from the forty-sixth to the seventh standard parallel would result in a loss to South Dakota of a valuable strip of fertile land, but such was better than the alternative.

Bennett's bill was pigeonholed, and when North and South Dakota were eventually admitted to the Union, the seventh standard parallel was designated as their common boundary. The simple designation of the seventh standard parallel as the boundary between the two states did not, however, solve all the problems that were involved. The seventh standard parallel, contrary to common assumption, was not a straight line from the eastern boundary of the territory to the Missouri River. Moreover, there were two seventh standard parallels in Dakota Territory prior to its division into states. Both were well defined and the Interior Department in Washington had endorsed and reported both of them.

The surveyor general of Dakota had prepared diagrams and explanations and had warned that failure to agree on the location of the seventh standard parallel would result in endless trouble and litigation. If one Dakota adopted one seventh standard parallel and the other Dakota another seventh standard parallel, the federal government could approve both. Depending on which parallel was used, one of the new states would gain or lose land. Dakotans in the southern counties objected to drawing the seventh standard parallel too far south because doing so would allow the northern counties to acquire many acres of land not belonging to them, including many school sections, which in the future would be a valuable asset to the state.

The confusion regarding the location of the seventh standard parallel arose because of a mistake made in the Minnesota surveyor general's office, according to General Beadle, who had been surveyor general for Dakota prior to becoming territorial superintendent of schools. It had been intended to base the survey of the seventh standard parallel across the Sisseton and Wahpeton Indian Reservation on the eastern edge of the territory on the fifth principal meridian base. Unfortunately, in the Minnesota surveyor general's office, a critical reference had been written as "miles and chains" when it should have been written as "chains and links." Consequently, the seventh standard parallel across the reservation was drawn about two and one-quarter miles south of where it should have been.

Should the seventh standard parallel, so located, be "extended due west" from this point to the Montana boundary, a sizeable amount of territory would be involved, and endless uncertainty, litigation, and hard feelings would result. More tempered accounts held that the seventh standard parallel was a clearly defined and acceptable line, except where it crossed the Sisseton and Wahpeton Indian Reservation. Nearing the Missouri River, the seventh standard parallel veered somewhat north of a due west course, but, otherwise, the parallel was a good line.

In any event, because of the confusion, the matter of where the seventh standard parallel was located had to be clarified. It was of utmost importance that the line be clearly defined and accepted as the definitive boundary between the states. People living along the line had to know whether they lived in North or South Dakota, and they needed to know to which state they owed their taxes. The location of the seventh standard parallel was also a matter of concern for the federal government. The proposed boundary would pass through such federal jurisdictions as Indian reservations, judicial districts, land office districts, and postal districts. As reported in the *New York Times* on March 5, 1889, national attention was being focused on the location of the elusive seventh standard parallel.

Locating the seventh standard parallel was a matter that occupied the attention of delegates to both the North and South Dakota constitutional conventions. A resolution was moved at the North Dakota constitutional convention that the Joint Commission that was to settle and adjust the indebtedness and divide the property of the territory also be empowered to fix temporarily the location of the seventh standard parallel until such time as the true line had been ascertained. In subsequent discussion on the resolution, some delegates declared that the convention would be exceeding its authority by doing so. The Omnibus Bill had provided that the southern boundary of North Dakota would be the seventh standard parallel, but the location of that parallel could be fixed only by the federal government.

Others objected to the convention's trying to determine the location of the parallel, even on a temporary basis, because more time would be spent debating the issue than would be required to write and adopt a state constitution. Over all objections, however, the resolution was passed. The Joint Commission was instructed to fix temporarily the location of the seventh standard parallel.

In South Dakota, when the matter of fixing the seventh standard parallel was raised in the constitutional convention, it was referred to the Committee on Name, Boundaries, and Seat of Government. After due deliberation, the committee concluded that the Omnibus Bill had not authorized the constitutional conventions of North and South Dakota to determine "what constitutes the true Seventh Standard Parallel." The committee recommended that no action be taken, a recommendation that was approved by the convention as a whole. The members of the Joint Commission, after deliberation, also concluded that they had no power to decide where the seventh standard parallel lay. The decisions of the constitutional conventions and the Joint Commission that neither had the authority to locate the seventh standard parallel left an open field for enterprising individuals who sought to realize both economic and political fortunes. Such an individual was Richard F. Pettigrew.

According to Charles A. Smith in his history of Minnehaha County, South Dakota, Pettigrew was one of the most "spectacular and outstanding 'boosters' the city [Sioux Falls] and state has ever known." Pettigrew was born in Ludlow, Vermont, on July 23, 1848, and moved with his parents to Wisconsin in 1854. He taught school for a time and then hired out as a chainman in a surveying party. He came to Sioux Falls, Dakota Territory, in 1869 and almost immediately grasped the possibilities and opportunities afforded by the area to someone possessed with his foresight and drive. He did extensive surveying work in Minnehaha, Moody, and Brookings counties before returning to Wisconsin to study law.

When Pettigrew returned to Sioux Falls after obtaining his law degree, he resumed surveying and also entered politics. He served successive terms in the territorial legislature and was also elected delegate from Dakota Territory to Congress in 1880. He was independent, outspoken, and aggressive. He was also, according to many accounts, "ever on the alert to promote South Dakota's interests, institutions and development." And one such occasion to promote South Dakota's interests, as well as his own, was the need to survey and mark the boundary between the twin states of North and South Dakota. Pettigrew's endeavors were successful in part due to his own efforts, but also due to the aid given him by well-placed friends and legislative colleagues in Washington.

Because the North Dakota and South Dakota constitutional conventions and the Joint Commission named to act on behalf of the two states could not fix the seventh standard parallel without exceeding the authority granted them in the Enabling Act, it devolved on the federal government to act. The state boundary had to be determined, surveyed, fixed, and marked as quickly as possible, and the boundary, once fixed, had to be one that all parties could accept. Minor adjustments could be made over time by a process of cooperation and accommodation, but, beginning at the Minnesota border, the seventh standard parallel had to be located and extended "due west" to the Montana border. Just as the matter of statehood for Dakota Territory had been debated in consecutive sessions of the United States Congress, now the location of the boundary between the two states became an issue during the first session of the Fifty-first Congress.

Oscar S. Gifford, no stranger to Washington legislative halls and now the duly elected representative from the new state of South Dakota, on December 18, 1889, introduced a bill (H.R. 792) in the

House of Representatives "to authorize the Secretary of the Interior to survey and mark the boundary line between the states of North and South Dakota. . . . " The bill was read for the first and second times, referred to the Committee on Public Lands, and ordered printed. Gifford was in a position to influence the passage of H.R. 792 because he was on two important House Committees – Public Buildings and Grounds and also Indian Affairs – and the proposed boundary between the two states ran through Indian reservations both east and west of the Missouri River.

Two days earlier, on December 16, Pettigrew introduced a bill (S. 1355) in the United States Senate "to authorize the Secretary of the Interior to survey and mark the boundary line between the States of North Dakota and South Dakota. . . . " The bill was read twice by its title and referred to the Committee on Public Lands. Pettigrew's bill contained an unfortunate, and, for Pettigrew, an uncharacteristic omission, a weakness that was quickly noted by Senator Algernon S. Paddoch of Nebraska, who was on the Senate Committee on Public Lands, the committee to which S. 1355 was referred. Pettigrew's bill did not mention the seventh standard parallel.

Paddoch's committee reported adversely on Pettigrew's bill, and action on the bill was postponed indefinitely. Thereupon Paddoch on March 12, 1890, introduced his own bill (S. 3089). Senate bill 3089 was only slightly, but significantly, different from senate bill 1355. Paddoch's more carefully crafted bill would authorize the secretary of the interior to survey and mark "the seventh standard parallel" between North and South Dakota and fix it as the boundary between the two states.

The text of the bill read in part:

> Be it enacted, etc., That the Secretary of the Interior be, and is hereby authorized to cause to be surveyed, ascertained, and distinctly marked, by suitable and permanent monuments the seventh standard parallel of permanent surveys between the States of North Dakota and South Dakota, such survey to conform in all respects to the general system of public surveys of the United States.

Section two of the bill provided "that for the purpose of carrying out the provision of this act, the sum of $25,000, or so much thereof as may be necessary, is hereby appropriated, out of any moneys in the Treasury not otherwise appropriated."

Paddoch's membership on the Senate Committee on Public Lands afforded him the opportunity to influence the passage of the bill. On April 3, 1890, it was Pettigrew's good fortune to be placed on the same committee, to replace Senator Henry W. Blair from New Hampshire, who had been excused from the committee.

Paddoch's bill was reported out of committee, reported to the Senate without amendment, passed by the Senate on March 18, 1890, and referred to the House Committee on Public Lands. It was fortunate for the proponents of the bill that South Dakota also had a person in the lower house who was well placed to ensure that the bill received favorable treatment. That person was John A. Pickler, recently elected Representative from South Dakota and a member of the House Committee on Public Lands.

John A. Pickler, South Dakota's representative to Congress in 1890. South Dakota: Pictorial-Biographical.

On May 7, 1890, Pickler's committee reported favorably on senate bill 3089. In House Report No. 1914, the committee members detailed reasons for supporting the bill and for recommending that it be passed. Wrote Congressman Pickler for the committee, succinctly if not grammatically:

> The Committee respectfully submit that it is important that this measure become a law without delay. It is important in defining the territorial jurisdiction of the courts, in describing the location of post offices, and that the citizens settling near the boundary line between the States of

> North Dakota and South Dakota may be able to determine with certainty their location, and that the permanent boundary between said States may be fixed.

In the ensuing debate on S. 3089, Congressman William C. P. Breckinridge from Kentucky objected to the federal government's being involved in the survey of the Dakota boundary because it was his understanding that locating the boundary between two states had always been the responsibility of the states. Such had been the case when locating the boundaries between Maryland and Virginia, between Tennessee and Kentucky, and between Delaware and Pennsylvania. Other Congressmen offered yet more examples of states that had undertaken the responsibility themselves of locating their mutual boundaries: Ohio and Pennsylvania and New York and New Jersey.

On September 4, 1890, in remarks to the House, Pickler spoke in defense of S. 3089 and explained why the federal government had to assume responsibility for the survey of the seventh standard parallel and fix it as the boundary between North and South Dakota. Both states had been formed from a territory recently under the jurisdiction of the United States government. Moreover, because the federal government had so much at stake, it would not do to allow the states to assume the responsibility of locating the boundary that separated them.

Breckinridge dismissed Pickler's arguments and pointed out that "when a Territory becomes a State of the Union it becomes equal to every other State in its privileges, its responsibilities, and its duties. It is the equal of every other State whether they were in the original thirteen or not." And, he concluded, "the boundaries of the States are State matters and not national matters, and they ought to be run by the States themselves." Even when Breckinridge eventually withdrew his objections to the passage of the bill, he wanted on record his prediction that the bill would set a bad precedent.

A second major objection raised to the passage of senate bill 3089 was that it would require the federal government, and not the states of North and South Dakota, to pay the cost of surveying and marking their mutual boundary. Congressman James Buchanan of New Jersey thought that North and South Dakota should bear the expense of the survey and marking because in the past this expense had been borne by the states themselves. That an appropriation was involved also provided opponents of the bill, such as Joseph G. Cannon of Illinois, with the opportunity to attempt killing it through the artful use of parliamentary techniques. Congressman Benton McMillin of Tennessee tried to stifle debate on S. 3089 by suggesting that a bill involving rivers and harbors be considered in its place.

Pickler's arguments that the federal government, and not the states of North and South Dakota, should assume the responsibility and cost for conducting the survey apparently influenced his fellow Congressmen because the bill passed the House on September 17, 1890. Pickler's strongest point, and one that none of the bill's opponents could refute, was that the seventh standard parallel was "an imaginary line" and that the federal government had a vital interest in knowing where this line lay.

In bisecting the former Territory of Dakota, the seventh standard parallel ran through hundreds of thousands of acres of land still owned by the federal government and open to entry. Federal land officials had to administer this land and handle its transfer to private ownership. They had to know in which state the land lay so they would know which land office had jurisdiction over it.

For other reasons as well, those supporting the passage of S. 3089 held that logic and necessity were on their side. There were United States post offices and courts lying along this "purely imaginary" line, and it would be impossible to determine the extent of jurisdiction of any of them until the

Richard F. Pettigrew, South Dakota's first senator.
South Dakota: Pictorial-Biographical.

seventh standard parallel had been surveyed and defined.

Pettigrew, new to the United States Senate but not to the give and take of politics, was also apparently instrumental in getting the federal government to assume the responsibility and the cost for surveying and marking the seventh standard parallel. The Sioux Falls *Daily Argus Leader* on October 1, 1890, noted that Sioux Falls was becoming known for its hailstorms, its divorce industry, and its "rustling senator." Another Sioux Falls newspaper, the *Daily Press,* described Pettigrew as "a leader who became such without any state prestige." The *Daily Press* applauded Pettigrew's accomplishments during his first year in the Senate. Because of Pettigrew's efforts, many bills favorable to the state's interests had been passed, and, also due to Pettigrew's efforts, "South Dakota [had] broken the record for new state appropriations."

It was not only hometown newspapers that praised the new senator. The *Daily Alert* in Jamestown, North Dakota, proclaimed that "Sioux Falls is being advertised handsomely by Pettigrew." The *Daily Fargo Forum* on March 16, 1892, after commenting on all the appropriations Pettigrew had secured for South Dakota, exclaimed, "That's a Senator that is a Senator." The Minneapolis *Tribune* attributed Pettigrew's popularity to his being "a fighter." He served the interests of his constituents and secured recognition and appropriations for his state. Perhaps, admitted the *Tribune* writer, Pettigrew was not always right, but he possessed qualities that made him a valuable senator from a new state. Even his political opponents admired his grit, perseverance, and consistency.

Pettigrew's supporters, much of the newspaper press, many of his constituents, and even many of his opponents credited him with having secured from the federal government the appropriation of $25,000 to pay for surveying and marking the seventh standard parallel as the boundary between North and South Dakota. (In 1892 he secured a slightly smaller appropriation to survey and mark the boundary between South Dakota and Nebraska.) Pettigrew built a strong case for the survey's being the responsibility of the federal government rather than the states of North and South Dakota. One of his main points bears repeating.

It had been customary for states when they entered the Union to establish their boundaries at their own expense. Pettigrew argued persuasively that in the case of the Dakotas, however, the boundary passed through extensive Indian reservations, over which the federal government had exclusive jurisdiction. The Sisseton and Wahpeton Indian Reservation extended across the seventh standard parallel on the extreme eastern end of the boundary between North and South Dakota. West of the Missouri River, the Standing Rock Reservation extended over almost half of the distance along the parallel between the river and the Montana border.

Pettigrew's arguments had a telling effect. Newspapers, from major dailies like the *Daily Argus Leader* of Sioux Falls and the Minneapolis *Tribune* to small weeklies like the Ipswich *Leaflet,* credited him with securing the federal appropriation for surveying and marking the seventh standard parallel so that the new states of North and South Dakota would not have to bear the cost. It was, according to the Aberdeen *Daily News,* yet another example of Pettigrew's interest in the welfare of the people of South Dakota. He did not miss an opportunity to secure an appropriation that would benefit his constituents or save the state money.

Senate bill 3089 was eventually passed by the United States House of Representatives, and on September 17, 1890, the speaker of the House signed the bill. A day later, on September 18, it was signed in the Senate by the vice-president. President Benjamin Harrison signed the bill into law on September 25, 1890. The United States secretary of the interior thereupon undertook to carry out the provisions of the law by advertising for bids to survey and mark the seventh standard parallel from the Minnesota border on the east to the Montana border on the west.

Chapter 3

Surveying the Public Domain

"The surveyor's lot is not a happy one!"
(with apologies to W. S. Gilbert)

The surveyor general was the official in the Treasury Department who was at first responsible for both the measurement and the dispensing of public land. As new land districts were opened, however, each requiring the appointment of a surveyor general, it became necessary to establish an agency to handle the nation's increasing real estate business. On April 25, 1812, a law was approved establishing the General Land Office within the Treasury Department. The official in charge was known as the commissioner of the General Land Office. The commissioner's responsibilities were to superintend the land districts, each the size of what later became one or two states, and supervise the surveyors general who were in charge of the land districts. In 1849, the General Land Office was transferred to the newly established Department of the Interior and placed under the supervision of the secretary of the interior.

When Dakota Territory was organized in March 1861, George D. Hill was appointed the first surveyor general of the District of Dakota. The surveyor general's office was located at Yankton until July 2, 1883, when it was moved to Huron. When Dakota Territory was divided into two states in 1889, it was necessary to establish offices of surveyor general in each of the two new states of North and South Dakota. Such was the purpose of a bill (S. 1984) that was introduced in the first session of the Fifty-first Congress on January 14, 1890.

House Report No. 1080, which supported the passage of S. 1984, noted that there were about 17.5 million acres of unsurveyed public lands in North Dakota and about 24.5 million acres of unsurveyed public lands in South Dakota. These millions of acres of public land had to be surveyed because, as Everett Dick noted in his book *The Lure of the Land,* "second in importance only to the preservation of life on the frontier was the security of ownership of one's tract of land, which required an effective system of surveys."

Senate bill 3089, passed during the first session of the Fifty-first Congress, had charged the secretary of the interior with the responsibility of insuring that the seventh standard parallel between the new states of North and South Dakota was correctly surveyed and distinctly marked, "such survey to conform in all respects to the general system of public surveys of the United States." The "general system of public surveys," to which S. 3089 referred, was that laid down in the Ordinance of 1785.

Considering the size of the area that eventually became the United States, the amount of public land owned by the federal government, the value of this land as a source of income to the government, and the need to transfer this land to private ownership, the Ordinance of 1785 is among the most important and far-reaching statutes in American history. This ordinance, which set precedents that the United States followed in its expansion all the way to the Pacific, provided for a plan of public land surveys and sales.

In disposing of the public domain, the Continental Congress had to choose between two established systems: the New England practice of surveying lands before settlement and selling them in orderly blocks, or the southern custom of "indiscriminate location and subsequent survey," by which a settler was allowed to

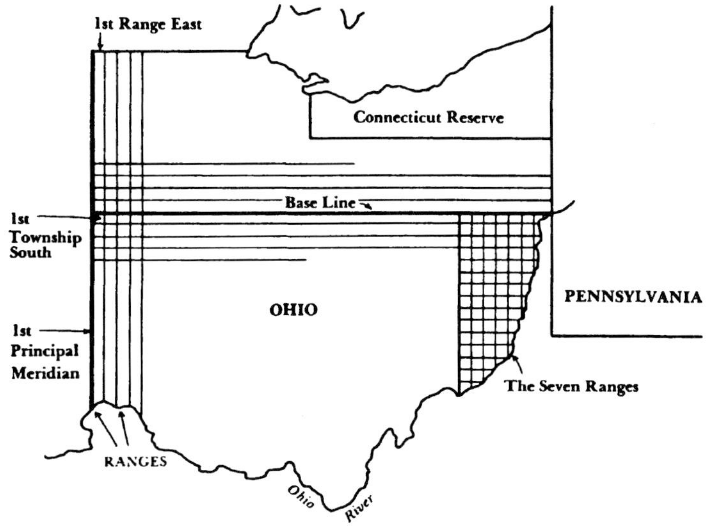

An Ordinance of 1785 providing for the national surveying system established the base line, or geographer's line, due west from the point at which the Ohio River intersects the western boundary of Pennsylvania. The first principal meridian later became the boundary between Ohio and Indiana. To accommodate settlers who were streaming into the area, the seven ranges were marked off in an exception to the normal surveying procedures.

Illustration depicting base lines, principal meridians, ranges, and townships. The advantage of this system is that a parcel of land can be located with reference to a range, township, and section number. Reprinted from The Lure of the Land, *by Everett Dick, by permission of University of Nebraska Press. Copyright © 1970 by the University of Nebraska Press.*

purchase a warrant, lay out his plot where he wished, and then have it surveyed.

Among the strengths of the New England system was that it did away with conflicting titles and endless litigation. Settlers were also assured that their lives and property would be protected as they moved westward in compact tiers. A weakness of the system, however, was that immigration might be discouraged because poor land had to be purchased along with the good. Frontiersmen favored the southern system because they could avoid poor land by laying out irregularly shaped plots. The weaknesses of the latter system were that it bred a welter of conflicting titles and surveying the irregular-shaped plots could not be done accurately.

The matter was debated in Congress between 1781 and 1785, when a committee was established to make a recommendation regarding the disposal of public land. The result, which was a compromise in order to satisfy landseekers in both the south and north, was the Ordinance of 1785, adopted on May 20 of that year. This "Ordinance for ascertaining the mode of disposing of Lands in the Western Territory" outlined the means of disposal of the lands ceded by individual states to the United States.

The Land Ordinance of 1785 provided that all government-owned lands would be divided into townships six miles square. Townships, in turn, would be subdivided into thirty-six numbered sections, each containing one square mile or 640 acres. Each section could be further subdivided into four quarter sections of 160 acres each.

At first, the sections in each township were to be numbered from one to thirty-six, beginning with number one in the southeast corner and running from south to north (from bottom to top) in each column (each rectangle of sections one mile wide and six miles long). In 1796 the system of numbering was changed. The law now read: "The sections shall be numbered, respectively, beginning with number 1 in the northeast section, and proceeding west and east, alternately through the township with progressive numbers till the thirty-sixth be completed."

Congress reserved four sections in each township for subsequent disposal and set section sixteen in each township aside for the support of schools—a remarkable feature of the ordinance at a time when public schools were rare. (Beginning with Oregon's admission to the Union in 1848, each state received section thirty-six as well.) This rectangular survey system made possible the orderly and efficient transfer of land from the public domain to private ownership without the endless litigation that would have resulted had everyone been allowed to select the land of his choice and mark it as he chose. A prospective settler could obtain a specific, previously surveyed

6 Miles (each side)

36	30	24	18	12	6
35	29	23	17	11	5
34	28	22	16	10	4
33	27	21	15	9	3
32	26	20	14	8	2
31	25	19	13	7	1

The methods of numbering sections as provided for in the Ordinance of 1785 (left) and the act of 1796 (below, left). The latter system has remained in effect to the present day.

6 Miles (each side)

6	5	4	3	2	1
7	8	9	10	11	12
18	17	16	15	14	13
19	20	21	22	23	24
30	29	28	27	26	25
31	32	33	34	35	36

Township

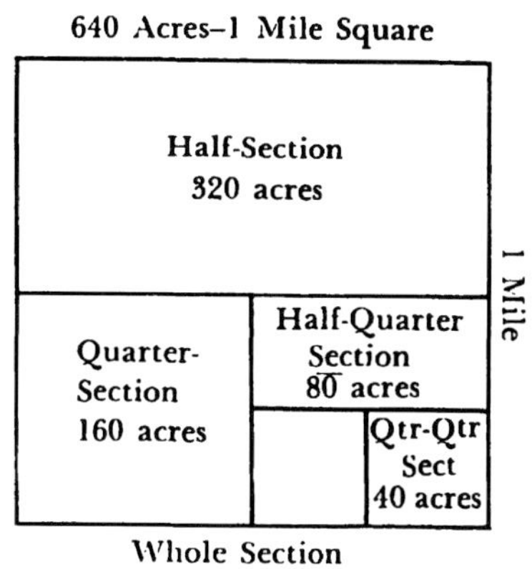

SYSTEM OF PUBLIC LANDS SURVEY – 1796

Illustration depicting the numbering of sections in a township and their division into parcels of 320, 160, 80, and 40 acres. Reprinted from The Lure of the Land, *by Everett Dick, by permission of University of Nebraska Press. Copyright © 1970 by the University of Nebraska Press.*

tract identified by range, township, and section number.

The 1785 land ordinance required surveyors of public land to measure lines with a chain, mark the line by "chaps on the trees," and describe the line on a plat. Surveyors were also required to describe the terrain; ascertain the quality of the soil; and note all water courses, mountains and "other remarkable and permanent things" over which the survey lines passed, including those that were manmade.

When settlement or expediency made it necessary that new portions of the land district be surveyed, Congress appropriated funds for the purpose. The surveyor general let contracts to deputy surveyors, who in turn went into the field and "ran" the survey lines. Deputy surveyors were required to sign a convenant by which they agreed, for a stipulated sum, to conduct the survey according to the prescribed methods as laid down in the survey manuals, make the plats, and record their description of the land. Deputy surveyors and their assistants – consisting of chainmen, flagmen or axmen, and moundmen – took solemn oaths, recorded in the deputy surveyor's notebook, to discharge their duties faithfully. The deputy surveyor was also required to furnish bonds that would be forfeited if the work were not completed or if it were poorly or carelessly done.

Contracts to "run" the township lines were customarily let first, and subsequent contracts were let to subdivide the townships into sections and quarter sections. This system made it absolutely necessary that each contractor do accurate work. Should the surveyor who ran the township lines not measure off a full six miles, there would not be sufficient area on which subsequently to measure off thirty-six full sections one mile square.

Township corners were established six miles apart, and section corners were established eighty chains, or one mile, apart. All corners had to be marked. A tree could serve to mark a corner if it stood on the exact spot where a corner was to be established. Otherwise, a post could be set at the "true corner," and two "witness" or "bearing" trees could be marked and their descriptions and distances from the true corner noted in the surveyor's field notes. When a tree was used to mark a corner, it was blazed and the numbers of the range, township, and section were scribed into the blaze with a scribing tool. Corners were first marked with charred stakes, posts, and mounds. Later contracts provided for mark-

Illustration depicting the use of stones, pits, and mounds with which to mark corners. From Instructions of the Commissioner of the General Land Office to the Surveyors General (1881).

ing corners with marked stones. Some of these stakes and stones now lie some distance beneath the surface, and surveyors must locate them when establishing or re-establishing property lines.

At section corners, surveyors were to set a post and dig pits eighteen inches wide, two feet long, and at least twelve inches deep, a distance of six feet from the post. The sides of the pits were usually oriented to the cardinal directions. The earth from the pits was used to form the mound around the post. Township corners were marked with larger mounds of earth and pits. The post used to mark the corner was four inches square and extended two feet above the ground. Notches and identification marks on the post had red chalk rubbed in them to make them more readily discernible.

It was once recommended that surveyors plant seeds at corners so that in time they would be marked with brush or useful trees. This practice was later discontinued, however, because animals, both domestic and wild, obliterated the corners by breaking the posts and trampling the mounds when they sought relief in the brush and trees from bothersome insects and the sun's heat.

When properly made in the summer, the mound was an excellent means by which to mark a corner. Prairie sod was cut and placed over the mound of loose dirt where, if rainfall were sufficient, it continued to grow. If the mound were built when the ground was frozen, however, the excavation had to be hacked out with a pickax and the sod would not take root. As a result, the mound was flattened by repeated rains and eventually disappeared.

A surveyor sometimes made a temporary mark at a corner, intending to return when the ground had thawed so he could construct a mound according to regulations. But he sometimes failed to return and fulfill his intentions or forgot where he had been working. Or perhaps the temporary marker had disappeared, and his conscience did not trouble him to the extent that he expended the time and effort necessary to determine the location again.

On the plains, where there were few trees, and especially west of the 98th meridian where posts were practically impossible to obtain, surveyors buried marked stones at township corners. When stones could not be found, surveyors were instructed to bury a quantity of charcoal for memorials. Charcoal is admirably suited for this purpose because it is remarkably impervious to moisture and can remain in the ground for decades without decaying.

The extreme difficulty that surveyors encountered on the plains to obtain wood of any kind with which to comply with regulations encouraged some to interpret the regulations loosely. Everett Dick recounted the story of one enterprising surveyor who

The Gunter's chain, also referred to as the surveyor's chain, invented by Sir Edmund Gunter in 1620. The Gunter's chain consists of 100 pieces of steel rod linked together with small rings. Its total length is 66 feet. Much of the public land in the United States was measured with the Gunter's chain. Legault/McMaster/Marlett, Surveying: An Introduction to Engineering Measurements, *© 1956, p. 43. Reprinted by permission of Prentice-Hall, Inc., Englewood Cliffs, NJ.*

rationalized that the absence of wood allowed him to make a substitution. He stuck a burned matchstick in the ground and swore that he had followed regulations by setting "a charred stick of the best available timber."

Before the advent of modern, electronic equipment, surveyors measured distances by means of the Gunter's, or surveyor's, chain. In chain measure, 7.92 inches equal 1 link; 100 links, or 66 feet, equal 1 chain; and 80 chains equal 1 mile. Washington furnished each surveyor general with a standard chain which he kept in his office. After 1841, possibly because it had been discovered that the standard chain at the surveyor general's office at Cincinnati was two inches too long, provision was made for an examiner of surveyors general. An inspector from the General Land Office was required to carry an accurate chain and to correct variations in the chains at the various offices of the surveyors general.

The surveyor general furnished each deputy surveyor with three chains: a standard chain, which he carried in his baggage, and two field chains, with which he made the actual measurements in the field. Before setting out to execute his surveying contract, the surveyor adjusted his standard chain with that kept by the surveyor general in his office. Every morning, before beginning the day's work, the surveyor was required to adjust the field chain he was going to use that day to his standard chain, which had been adjusted to the chain in the office of the surveyor general.

Everett Dick in his book *The Lure of the Land* has the following description of a survey crew at work:

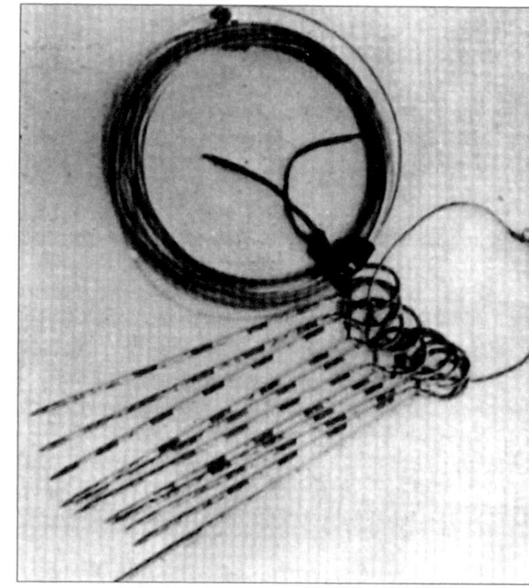

A steel tape and taping pins, which are also known as chain pins or chaining arrows. Because of its many wearing surfaces, the Gunter's chain will continue to increase in length as it is used. Consequently, all precise field measurements of horizontal lengths are made today with steel, metallic, or nonmetallic woven tapes. Legault/McMaster/Marlett, Surveying: An Introduction to Engineering Measurements, *© 1956, p. 47. Reprinted by permission of Prentice-Hall, Inc., Englewood Cliffs, NJ.*

It was the duty of two chainmen to measure the distance along the line indicated by the surveyor and to inform him when a half-mile had been measured so that the axmen, or moundmen as they were later called, might mark a corner. The forward chainman carried eleven tally pins, each rendered conspicuous by having a piece of red cloth tied in the ring at its top. He stuck a pin in the ground after he had stretched the chain for a

North Dakota Geological Survey camp, showing tent and equipment similar to what Bates and his survey crew would have used. Elwyn B. Robinson Department of Special Collections, Chester Fritz Library, University of North Dakota.

measurement. When he had stuck the eleventh pin, he cried "Tally!" which was repeated by the other chainman, and each man registered the tally by slipping a button or leather ring on a string stretched from one of his front pockets to another. The rear chainman, who had collected the pins, now came up to the front, counted the pins to check against loss, and became the forward chainman for the next tally. Four tallies made a half-mile. With the chain taut, the exact spot where a pin had to be stuck was determined by a plumb bob. This was important when descending a hill since in order to keep the chain level the front end of the chain was held several feet above the ground while the pin was stuck.

While on the line during the day, the surveyor made rough notes, which he wrote up at night in ink. The notes had to include a description of all corners and the type of markers used to mark them. The surveyor was also required to record all topographical features visible from the survey line and the distances to them. He also had to record information on timberland, prairies, waterways, school houses, farm buildings, towns, mineral deposits, Indian villages, and such natural curiosities as caves and mounds. Finally, the surveyor had to describe the surface of the land – whether it was rolling, hilly, or broken – and classify the soil as first, second, or third class.

Surveying the vast tracts of public lands provided employment for surveyors – some of whom were qualified and many of whom were not; and granting surveying contracts was an attractive means by which politicians could repay political debts and reward

North Dakota Geological Survey camp, showing tent and equipment similar to what Bates and his survey crew would have used. Elwyn B. Robinson Department of Special Collections, Chester Fritz Library, University of North Dakota.

friends. Many surveyors were political appointees, men almost completely lacking in technical training who were selected without examinations of any kind. A person wanting a surveying contract could enter the profession, not by demonstrating his ability, but on the recommendation of a powerful political connection who attested to the candidate's ability and political qualifications.

As a result of this method of choosing surveyors and letting contracts, much costly and dishonest surveying was done. Stories abound of surveyors who did their work in their hotel rooms, in saloons, and even on the tops of moving trains. Needless to say, a vivid imagination was a tremendous asset to such a surveyor. Some fraudulent contractors sketched major waterways into maps of trackless deserts and showed mountainous tracts to be fertile prairie. Careless work became especially evident when lines were run subdividing a township and it was discovered that quarter sections contained more or less than the customary 160 acres.

When William Andrew Jackson Sparks, a native of Illinois, became commissioner of the General Land Office during the first Cleveland administration, he instituted a remarkable and vigorous improvement in the administration of his office. A man of high ideals and irreproachable honesty, he insisted on clean government and the enforcement of the laws. Among his first acts was to ask Congress to reform the surveying system. Among his recommendations were that surveyors be penalized for filing false survey returns, that permanent markers of iron and stone be used rather than mounds, and that a punishment be instituted for the removal of markings. He also asked Congress for an appropriation of money with which to pay for inspecting surveys before they were accepted.

That surveying contracts had been let to reward friends and repay political debts and that shoddy work had been done were attested to by an article in the *New York Times* on March 19, 1892. The General Land Office was investigating a number of allegedly crooked transactions in the surveying district of South Dakota. Land commissioner Thomas H. Carter had asked the surveyor general of South Dakota for a report on the alleged irregularities.

According to the allegations, surveying contracts had been let, then sublet, and paid for in advance. Men unfit, untrained, and under age had secured positions in surveyors' offices at handsome salaries. Capable men with long records of service had been dismissed to make room for favorites. Contractors did their private surveying work while being paid for official duties. Partiality had been shown to certain deputy surveyors. In short, a system of favoritism and jobbery had been established, much to the detriment of the public interest.

Affidavits sustaining the charges and affidavits tending to disprove them were to be forwarded to the office of the surveyor-general for South Dakota, Boetris H. Sullivan, who had been appointed to the office on July 18, 1889. It was Sullivan's responsibility to clear the record for his office and his surveying district. At best, it appeared that there had been loose and careless management. If the charges were true, if there had been irregularities in granting surveying contracts, the authorities would have to make a general overhaul of the affairs of the district.

The conditions under which surveyors worked, however, were sometimes so difficult that errors were bound to occur no matter how conscientious or diligent the surveyor might be. Surveyors had to contend with unfriendly Indians, irate settlers, adverse weather conditions, rough terrain, dangerous beasts, bothersome insects, and personal discomfort.

Charles Clark was engaged in 1905 in surveying ten townships along the Cheyenne and White rivers in South Dakota. In an article entitled "Surveying on the Cheyenne," published in *South Dakota Historical Collections* in 1910, he detailed his experiences in the field. Wrote Clark, "the surveyor came with the advance guard of civilization. . . . " He dragged his mess wagon over impossible hills, through miles of viscid gumbo and across swollen rivers. He tramped miles with his heavy transit on his shoulder while he endured heat, cold, hunger, and thirst. He scaled cliffs where it was almost necessary to climb by using fingernails, and he balanced his tripod on the sharp crests of ridges where a slip of his foot would mean serious injury.

The surveyor's work, observed Clark, was "a daily struggle with unsubdued nature. . . . " Unremitting toil, rough fare, and constant exposure to every whim of the elements were the surveyor's daily portion. He had to possess both brain and brawn and carry in his head both the learning of a college man and the wisdom of a child of nature. Under adverse conditions the survey crew became weak, peevish, and quarrelsome. The flagman sulked and delayed the party. The chainmen stopped their work to quarrel. The cook produced undigestible messes in his smoky tent, and even the deputy surveyor was unsociable. The completion of the work, concluded Clark, was "largely a matter of dogged endurance with no enjoyment about it."

Thunderstorms often burst on the crew suddenly and at the most inopportune times. Hailstorms caught men miles from shelter and beat at them unmercifully. Tempests of rain and wind ripped tents and drove the men barefoot and half dressed into the night to chase the tents over the prairie. With the rain came the mosquitoes. In the prairie drains and depressions, they bred by the millions and rose in clouds to torment man and beast. The mosquitoes settled on the men in swarms during the day, getting into their noses and mouths and nearly strangling them. At night they followed the men into their tents and made sleep impossible.

The method followed by the survey crew was for the flagman to go ahead and "line in" to the signals of the surveyor and then mark the point of the new "set-up" of the transit with a small pile of sod. After the surveyor came the chainmen, measuring off the miles and pausing every chain length to thrust one of their iron pins into the ground and give their monotonous cry of "stick stuck." The moundmen followed with their spades, marking the corners sufficiently to be able to find them later when the time came to "build" them.

On one occasion, on level land, Clark remembered, the chainmen wanted to measure a mile in the record time of less than fifteen minutes. The record mile was never finished, however. The crew was caught in a terrible thunderstorm on a tableland that was the highest point for ten miles around. Lightning flashed all around them. The chainmen staggered under a shock as lightning struck their steel chain and numbed their arms to their elbows. The men hugged the ground until the lightning stopped. Then came the heavy, cold rain. The prairie was soon inches deep in water and the men were cut off from their camp by flooding streams. They were doomed to one of those experiences most dreaded by surveyors, a "night out." Fatigue and hunger were bearable, but cold and exposure could mean death.

Fires were common on the prairies and a terror to surveyors. When at work in the field, if the men smelled smoke or noticed flames and if the wind were blowing from the direction of the fire toward their camp, the crew would quit work and rush to the camp where they often had a hard fight in order to save their tents, equipment, and supplies. Often they had only feed sacks with which to beat out the flames.

Another torment with which surveyors had to contend while in the field was the dense growth of underbrush along the banks of streams, through which they had to cut in order to take their sightings. One deputy surveyor sent his notes to the surveyor general's office showing the point at which he had begun the day's work on a certain creek. After working all day to clear brush, the surveyor's only additional notation for that day was "same damned creek." It was only by dint of perseverance, sheer physical energy, and great powers of endurance that surveyors completed work under such trying conditions. Because of delays and unanticipated circumstances, their costs often exceeded the amount allowed them by the government under the terms of their contracts.

Suspicious and unfriendly Indians also added to the dangers faced by surveyors in the field. Some Indians opposed having surveys made across their lands, and on occasion they followed the survey party and obliterated the mounds or removed the posts and stones marking the corners. Surveys then had to be run a second time. Because some Indians used pegs with which to hold down their tents and because the surveyors were marking their line with pegs, these Indians feared that the white men were going to cover the entire country with a great tent and destroy their hunting grounds. Indians frequently threatened surveyors and sometimes killed them. It was common for Indians to destroy a surveyor's instruments because of their fear that they might lose their lands and homes as a result of the white man's work.

Zack T. Sutley was employed as a member of Thomas F. Marshall's survey party in 1878 near Redfield in Spink County, Dakota Territory. Indians, led by Chief Drifting Goose, were impeding the efforts of the surveyors to run their lines. The Indians tried to scare the surveyors out of the country, or, failing that, to provoke the surveyors to some act of violence that would justify the Indians' driving them out with force.

While the survey party was camped on the James River east of the present site of Ashton, Sutley, dismissed from the party for some reason, started on horseback for Yankton. Sutley had gone only a few miles when he stopped to water his horse at a small stream. Suddenly a band of Indians appeared and began to threaten him. Sutley quickly mounted his horse and began racing away, but his horse stepped into a hole and both horse and rider were thrown to the ground. In an instant the Indians were on him with knives drawn. They cut every stitch of clothing from him including his boots. The Indians then turned Sutley loose, but amused themselves by firing at him with their rifles, all the while barely missing him, until he had ridden out of range. Sutley returned to Marshall's camp so overcome with fright and fatigue that he was unable to speak or stand.

Charles H. Bates, who secured the contract to survey and mark the seventh standard parallel that serves as the boundary between North and South Dakota, was a deputy surveyor who after 1870 was engaged in surveying the public lands in Dakota Territory, both east and west of the Missouri River. In 1901 he was running a survey on the Pine Ridge Indian Reservation in southwestern South Dakota. Bates' experiences were described in an article by S. J. Goodfellow, "South Dakota's Early Surveys," published in 1910 in *South Dakota Historical Collections.*

Along the White River and White Clay Creek lived Indians who opposed the survey because they knew that it heralded the approach of the allotment of the lands in severalty. They destroyed the corners and markers whenever possible and warned the surveying party off the land. Bates' crew had for protection only one worn-out shotgun.

On one occasion, Bates sent the teamster with the supply wagon down a dim trail through a pine-studded canyon towards the valley below while the rest of the survey party were at work over the hills. About an hour later, the driver returned and informed Bates that the trail did not extend to the valley. A few days later, the fellow sheepishly admitted to Bates that the trail indeed extended to the valley, but that the way had been blocked by a very large and determined Indian woman brandishing an ax. Her actions indicated plainly enough that he was to go back the same way he had come—and quickly. He had been only too ready to obey her command.

Surveying the public domain was never easy work, and it was made the more difficult and frustrating when the elements did not cooperate. Bates and Sutley had a contract to survey for the Northern Pacific Railroad west of Bismarck in 1879. Early in the spring, before the ice on the Missouri River had broken up, the men went to Bismarck and carried the eleventh and twelfth standard parallels across the river on the ice and established corners on the west side of the river. By crossing on the ice, they avoided having to use triangulation to determine the width of the river.

The Northern Pacific was building west from the Missouri River through country underlaid with coal. Because there were so many minerals in the ground, the men could not use a magnetic-needle compass and consequently had to run all lines with a solar compass. When the sun was not shining, the work went slowly and the men spent a good deal of time in camp playing cards. Their favorite game was "seven-up," and the stakes were often coal banks, for some member of the crew would locate a new one almost every day. Because of Sutley's luck at finding coal banks and at playing cards, he once owned thirty coal banks. Coal banks were so numerous, however, that the men considered them of little value and consequently did not bother to file claims to them nor for the land on which they were located.

One Sunday a Mr. Cunningham from Yankton, who had a grading contract for the railroad, visited the surveyors' camp. Bates offered the visitor a drink of whiskey from the supply they carried for medicine and as an antidote against snakebite. A few days later, a man from the grading crew came riding wildly into the surveyors' camp and asked for a pint of whiskey for one of the graders who had been bitten by a rattlesnake. Bates and his men made fun of the fellow for thinking that they would be so gullible as to part with a pint of whiskey on the grounds of such an obvious fabrication.

Thinking better of it afterwards, however, Sutley mounted a horse and took a pint of whiskey to the grading camp. There he found that a worker had indeed been bitten by a rattler. The man's entire body was covered with blotches caused by the poison, and his hand, where the snake had struck, was terribly swollen. His friends had him buried in mud up to his mouth and nose to relieve his discomfort and to counteract the effects of the venom. After several small doses of the whiskey, the man began to feel better and the blotches began to disappear. A few days later he was taken from the mud—and eventually he recovered.

In rough country, every chain the surveyors measured presented a challenge. Bates commented that when a man was carrying heavy tools or a transit, especially over rugged terrain, any beauties of the landscape were lost on him because he had to concentrate constantly on how to run a straight line over terrain that was so rough as to be almost impassable.

Rough terrain, unfriendly Indians, bad weather – all could delay a surveyor's work and put him behind schedule. In 1890 a very religious young deputy surveyor in South Dakota realized that in order to finish the survey within the period allowed by his contract, he would have to work on Sunday. Before doing so, he thought it only prudent to wait until he had received instructions from the surveyor general. He asked his superior specifically whether it would be permissible to take celestial observations on Sunday. The surveyor general, with all due tact because of the seriousness of the request, assured the conscientious deputy surveyor that of all days in the week, there were none better suited to taking celestial observations than Sunday.

After undergoing the experiences and enduring the hardships they did while surveying the public lands, the men of the survey parties became callous to tribulation, and they accepted their lot, according to Charles Clark, with "the grim stoicism of a tortured Indian and the patient resignation of a martyr." The surveyor's place in American history must be recognized and appreciated, for the prairies and hills across which he ran his surveys were dotted with corners that would eventually mark the boundaries of homesteads and farms.

Chapter 4

The Boundary Monuments

"And the building of the wall of it was of jasper."
Revelation 21:18

As passed by the United States Congress and signed into law by President Benjamin Harrison on September 25, 1890, senate bill 3089 authorized the secretary of the interior "to cause to be surveyed, ascertained, and distinctly marked by suitable and permanent monuments, the seventh standard parallel of public surveys between the States of North Dakota and South Dakota, such survey to conform in all respects to the general system of public surveys of the United States." Congress appropriated $25,000, "or so much thereof as may be necessary," to defray the costs of the project.

William M. Stone, acting commissioner of the General Land Office, in a letter to the secretary of the interior dated October 1, 1890, wrote that because the survey had to be "carefully and accurately made" and the boundary "marked by conspicuous monuments of the most durable material . . . " the work should be entrusted only to "a thoroughly competent and trustworthy surveyor" whose professional reputation had been firmly established and whose integrity was above reproach. He believed that the project could be completed for considerably less than the $25,000 that had been appropriated for it.

Richard F. Pettigrew, newly elected senator from South Dakota and an experienced surveyor, in a letter to the secretary of the interior dated September 18, 1890, recommended that the boundary line be run astronomically and marked every mile with stone monuments ten inches square and seven feet long with half their length planted firmly in the earth. Pettigrew also stated that almost indestructible stone, which would make "most excellent and lasting monuments," was available from quartzite quarries in the vicinity of Sioux Falls, South Dakota. The General Land Office approved of the recommendations that the boundary be marked with stone monuments, but suggested that the monuments be placed every one-half mile instead of at intervals of one mile, as Pettigrew had suggested.

According to the specifications for the survey and marking of the boundary line between North and South Dakota, published by the General Land Office in March 1891,

> The Initial Point of the boundary between the States of North and South Dakota is the intersection of the seventh standard parallel north, of the 5th Principal Meridian System, with the main channel of the Bois des Sioux River [which forms the boundary between Minnesota and the two Dakotas]. The approximate geographical position of the Initial Point is in latitude 45° 55′ N. longitude 96° 33′ west.

From the initial point on the Minnesota boundary, the seventh standard parallel had been surveyed west about 11½ miles to the north boundary line of the Sisseton and Wahpeton Indian Reservation, across which an original survey of the standard parallel would have to be made – a distance of about 32¾ miles. At the time of statehood, the boundary between the two Dakotas across the reservation had been in some dispute, because within the limits of the reservation two seventh standard parallels had been laid down.

Carl C. P. Meyer had the first contract to produce the seventh standard parallel westward from the Minnesota boundary through the reservation, and he had made an error in his calculations as the result of incorrect figures furnished him by the office of the surveyor general of Minnesota. Consequently, he had located the line some two miles south of its proper position.

Once Meyer's error was discovered, his survey was disregarded. Subsequently, in 1872, Miles T. Wooley and Charles H. Bates had corrected Meyer's error by carrying up the lines from the sixth standard parallel and correctly locating the seventh standard parallel within the Sisseton and Wahpeton Indian Reservation. Satisfied that the corrected seventh standard parallel was the one that should be extended through the Indian reservation and westward to the Montana border, the secretary of the interior instructed the commissioner of the General Land Office by letter on December 3, 1890, to proceed with the survey and marking of the North and South Dakota boundary.

In 1874 deputy surveyor E. D. Palmer had taken up the corrected line of the seventh standard parallel and had carried it westward to the Missouri River, a distance of slightly more than 145 miles. Much of the seventh standard parallel between the Minnesota boundary and the Missouri River, therefore, with the exception of where it crossed the Sisseton and Wahpeton Indian Reservation, had already been surveyed by the time of statehood.

From the crossing of the Missouri River, the boundary was to be established by an original survey, according to the specifications, "as an extension of the 7th standard, on a true parallel of latitude," to the eastern boundary of Montana, a distance estimated to be 171¾ miles—much of it through federal land. The length of the entire boundary between the Dakotas, therefore, was estimated to be 361½ miles, of which 157 miles had been surveyed and were to

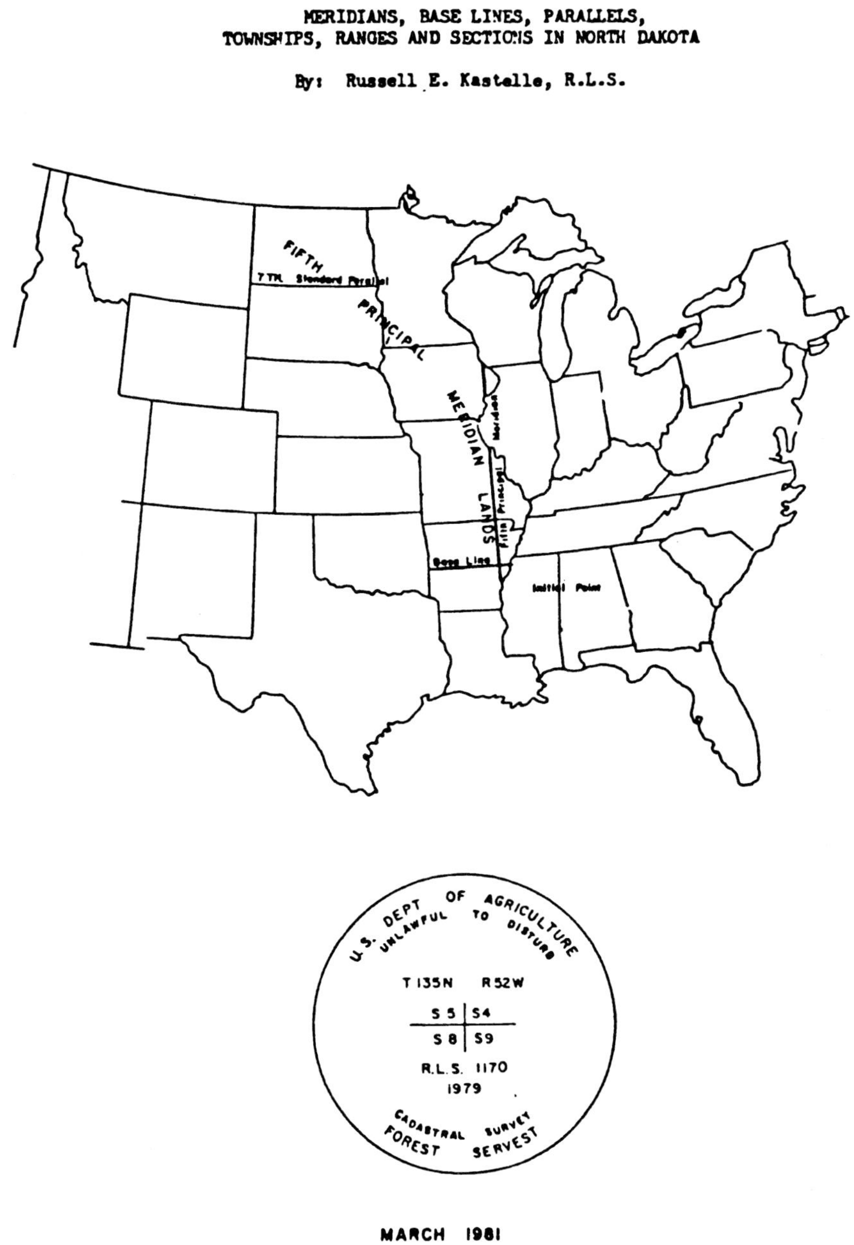

Sketch showing the land in the fifth principal meridian system, which includes all land in North Dakota. Russell E. Kastelle.

be retraced and 204½ miles that would require an original survey.

Land in the forty-eight contiguous states – with the exception of that in the thirteen original states and their land claims and in Texas – is located with reference to meridians, base lines, parallels, ranges, townships, and sections. And all land in North Dakota is located with reference to the initial point for the fifth principal meridian. (South Dakota has land in the sixth principal meridian and in the Black Hills meridian systems.) Russell E. Kastelle, Registered Land Surveyor from Breckenridge, Minnesota, has written a helpful summary of how the initial point for the fifth principal meridian was established and how land in North Dakota is located with reference to it.

Prospect K. Robbins began the survey of the fifth principal meridian on October 27, 1815, by setting a post "at the extremity of the point of land formed by the junction of the Arkansas and Mississippi Rivers." From this point, he proceeded due north and on November 10, 1815, he intersected a survey line that had been begun by Joseph Brown, another surveyor, who had begun his survey at the intersection of the St. Francis and Mississippi rivers. The intersection of these two lines was at 91° 03′ 42″ west longitude and 34° 44′ 00″ north latitude.

This point, which by chance fell in a swampy area in east central Arkansas about sixty-five miles east of Little Rock, is the initial point for the fifth principal meridian. The north-south line run by Robbins was named the "fifth principal meridian" because it was the fifth such line that was established in the United States government surveys. The east-west line run by Brown was the base line for the fifth principal meridian.

As the survey of the public domain was extended north and west from the initial point, shorter guide meridians were randomly established to compensate for the curvature of the earth and to facilitate the surveying of the specific areas of the country that were being developed. Consequently, all of the lands that were surveyed under the fifth principal meridian system were not surveyed in an orderly fashion. Surveying and opening land for settlement depended in part on when Indians ceded the land and when railroads were built that required surveys of their rights of way.

Additional base lines, called correction lines and later standard parallels, were run east and west at twenty-four mile intervals. The standard parallel numbering system used in North Dakota was carried over from the Minnesota surveys, the baseline in Minnesota being the Minnesota-Iowa border. The standard parallels in both Minnesota and North Dakota are numbered from that line. According to Kastelle, there is no direct mathematical relationship between the numbering of geographical parallels and survey parallels, nor is there any direct mathematical relationship between the numbering of geographical longitude meridians and survey principal or guide meridians. Any mathematical similarity in the numbering of these lines is only coincidental.

The survey meridians and parallels formed large rectangular tracts of land twenty-four miles square. The meridians and base lines were surveyed first; the township lines were run later. These lines were intended to be run on true east-west or north-south directions and were usually run by highly skilled surveyors with considerable emphasis on accuracy. Surveyors were instructed to make periodical astronomical observations on the sun or stars for the purpose of determining the true directions.

According to the specifications laid down by the Ordinance of 1785, each township is six miles square, and numbering in the fifth principal meridian system begins with number one at the initial base line in Arkansas. The first township north of the seventh standard parallel – that is, the first tier of townships across the entire state of North Dakota – is township 129 north. In other words, the seventh standard parallel is 129x6 or approximately 774 miles north of the initial base line in Arkansas.

Each range, six miles wide, is numbered beginning with number one at the principal meridian and numbered from there east or west. The first township in the southeast corner of North Dakota is in range 47 west. The range designation indicates the east-west direction and the township designation indicates the north-south direction. Range 47 west is then 47x6 or approximately 282 miles west of the fifth principal meridian. Each township in North Dakota has its own township number north and range number west by which it can be identified. Within each township, each section has a number by which it can be identified.

The survey of the boundary between North and South Dakota was "to conform in all respects to the general system of public surveys of the United States." That is, the boundary would be surveyed according to the method laid down in the

At Sioux Falls, South Dakota, the Big Sioux River flows through spectacular outcroppings of quartzite. Photo taken prior to the flood of 1881, which washed away the "Lone Rock" located in the center foreground. R. E. Kolbe Dakota Collection.

Ordinance of 1785. The markings of the boundary, however, would be unique. No other state boundary in the nation is marked along its entire length by "conspicuous monuments of the most durable material" as is the boundary between North and South Dakota.

In southeastern South Dakota, along the Big Sioux River in Minnehaha and adjacent counties, lie large beds of quartzite or jasper. At Sioux Falls, South Dakota – hence the name "Sioux Falls quartzite" – and at Jasper, Minnesota – named after the stone – large outcroppings of quartzite are visible above ground. Near Dell Rapids, South Dakota, the perpendicular quartzite cliffs rise sixty feet into the air on both sides of the Big Sioux River. Major John Wesley Powell of the United States geological survey estimated the depth of the quartzite deposits in the Sioux Falls area to be between three and four hundred feet. South Dakota state geologist S. E. Todd in his report in 1894 put the depth at 1,500 feet.

Quartzite may be described as a metamorphic quartzite rock of intense hardness, colored by a natural chemical process and ferric oxide in various shades of pink, red, lavender, violet, delicate blue, and gray. Sioux Falls quartzite, seventh in hardness to diamond of precious and non-precious stone – chips of it will cut glass – is composed of over 97.5 percent silica (2.5 percent iron) fused, according to a report cited by Pettigrew, at 3,000°F. In tests conducted at the Chicago Hydraulic Works, Sioux Falls quartzite withstood pressures of 25,000 pounds to the square inch, twice that of ordinary granite. Pettigrew, in a letter to the commissioner of the General Land Office on September 29, 1890, cited tests showing that quartzite would withstand a pressure of 47,000 pounds to the square inch before being crushed.

The Hubbard Stone and Construction Company of Sioux Falls sent a number of two-inch cubes of Sioux Falls quartzite, both blue and pink, to the Bureau of Ordinance of the United States Navy to be tested for their ability to withstand crushing. Extracts from the reports (No. 1825 dated May 15, 1890), were published in a brochure advertising both the construction company and the superior qualities of quartzite. According to the report, "None of the samples showed any signs of weakness under a pressure of 85,000 lbs., which is the capacity of our testing machine. If further tests are required, it is suggested that cubes measuring one inch on a side be furnished." In accordance with the suggestion, the Hubbard Company sent samples of quartzite to the Watertown Arsenal for further tests.

Not only does quartzite withstand tremendous pressure without crumbling, exposure to neither weather nor running water nor heat will cause it to deteriorate. Pettigrew wrote to the commissioner of the General Land Office that quartzite monuments exposed to the elements for over twenty years showed no evidence of deterioration. The Big Sioux River has been flowing in its present course for about 10,000 years at Sioux Falls, yet the outcroppings of quartzite forming the falls have not worn away. Heat that would crumble sandstone, marble, or granite has no appreciable effect on quartzite.

Reports of tests conducted by the University of Wisconsin and by the Chicago Hydraulic Works, the former at Pettigrew's request, noted that Sioux Falls quartzite possessed the following qualities: (1) harder than granite, limestone, or sandstone; (2) more indifferent to heat than granite or limestone; (3) more indifferent to acid than granite or limestone; (4) takes as fine a polish as chalcedony; (5) extraordinarily rich and delicate in color; and (6) believed to combine beauty and strength more perfectly than any other stone in America.

Sioux Falls quartzite compared favorably with the finest Scotch granite because of its exceedingly fine grain and because it took a beautiful, glass-like finish that recommended its use for table tops, monuments, and columns. In short, according to its promoters, Sioux Falls quartzite was unexcelled in strength, durability, and beauty as a building stone.

For many reasons, Pettigrew had recommended to the secretary of the interior that stone monuments of conspicuous size be used to mark the boundary between North and South Dakota. A distinctly marked boundary would allow for easier location of land claims and also preclude difficulties between conflicting jurisdictions such as the courts, postal districts, and land offices. Stone monuments would last longer than iron posts and they would cost less. Iron markers would be too small, or if large enough to serve the purpose, too expensive.

Pettigrew was also speaking on behalf of the quarry industry in Sioux Falls and the surrounding area, however, when he championed the use of stone monuments to mark the boundary between North and South Dakota. Not without cause was Pettigrew known as a "fighter" and as South Dakota's "rustling senator." He also, according to the Jamestown *Daily Alert*, "handsomely advertised" Sioux Falls. And among the attributes of Sioux Falls that Pettigrew advertised was the budding quarry industry.

The quartzite monuments marking the boundary between North and South Dakota, believed Pettigrew, would be a

The Falls of the Big Sioux River in Sioux Falls, South Dakota, ca 1905. R. E. Kolbe Dakota Collection.

standing advertisement to the Sioux Falls stone industry. And it was because of the influence that he exerted as a United States senator that many of the nation's public buildings and the streets along which they stood were constructed from Sioux Falls quartzite. According to an article in the Sioux Falls *Daily Argus Leader* on September 12, 1890, the stone industry would be a valuable asset contributing to the growth and wealth of the city, providing the quarries were developed and advertised. There was no better way of advertising the product of the quarries than by shipping the stone throughout the United States. And wherever the stone was shipped, it should be labelled "Sioux Falls' Jasperite." The attention of every person seeing something constructed from quartzite would be drawn to Sioux Falls and its potential as a business, financial, and industrial center.

At the time of statehood of the two Dakotas, the quartzite industry in the Sioux Falls area was in its infancy, but promoters held out high hopes for it. Already hundreds of men were employed in a growing number of quarries, and one Sioux Falls stone company had shipped 8,400 cars of paving material—a total of 12,400,000 blocks. In the Sioux Falls *Daily Argus Leader* on July 18, 1890, the Sioux Falls Granite Company (Ltd.) advertised that the company dealt in building stone and paving blocks and specialized in rock face fronts for buildings. The company's main office was in Sioux Falls, but it also had offices in Chicago and Omaha.

Other quarries that had opened up within and near Sioux Falls by 1890 were Monarch Quarries, 3rd Street and French Avenue; Seney Quarry, 5th Street and River; Bennett Quarry, Weber Avenue and Madison Street; McGarraugh Quarry, Cliff Avenue and Arcadia Road; and Coats Quarry, on Block 7, Riverdale 2nd Addition. At the height of the stone industry, quarries were also opened at Rowena and in East Sioux Falls. An electric car line was constructed and operated between Sioux Falls and East Sioux Falls, primarily to serve the quarries. Quarries were also opened at Dell Rapids, South Dakota, and at Jasper, Minnesota.

The quartzite industry in Sioux Falls dates from the early 1880s. The large, six-story Queen Bee flour mill at the site of the falls was constructed in 1881 of quartzite blocks. J. H. Drake opened the Monarch quarry in Sioux Falls, and in 1884 he established a water-powered polishing works on the east side of the Big Sioux River south of McClellan Street. The first steps to pave the streets in Sioux Falls, which were almost impassable much of the year, were taken in the late spring of 1888, when the city council began discussing the relative merits of quartzite and other materials for the paving. Although the first cost of quartzite would be greater than that of other materials commonly used for paving, the durability of quartzite "and the fact that it would be a lasting advertisement of its admirable qualities for such purposes"

Rowena Quarry. Siouxland Heritage Museums, Sioux Falls, South Dakota.

convinced members of the city council to vote unanimously in favor of specifying quartzite for the city's first paving project – Phillips Avenue from 5th to 8th streets. The contract was let June 1, 1888.

The paving material used on Phillips Avenue was jasper and the curb was jasperite, a darker stone than the paving blocks. The contract price was $2.13 per square yard for the paving stone and $.70 per lineal foot for the curbing. When the paving project was completed, an authority on street paving pronounced it the finest street of paving in the United States. Almost impervious to wear, quartzite paving blocks, nevertheless, became polished with wear and, therefore, provided a slippery surface for horse traffic even when the horses were shod.

That he believed in the products he promoted is evidenced by Pettigrew's use of quartzite when constructing businesses and buildings in which he had a financial interest. The Queen Bee Mill has already been mentioned. In 1889, enlisting the support of Maine capitalists, Pettigrew incorporated the Sioux Falls Stock Yards Company, to establish a large packinghouse and stockyards on one thousand acres of land southwest of the city near the junction of Skunk Creek and the Big Sioux River. The massive, six-story building that housed the slaughtering operations was constructed of quartzite and it stood until 1939-1940, when it was razed as a WPA project. The stone was salvaged and used for construction elsewhere in Sioux Falls. The cornerstone, marked "1890," rests today near the north entrance of the Pettigrew Museum in Sioux Falls.

Drake Quarry. Siouxland Heritage Museums, Sioux Falls, South Dakota.

Early in his senatorial career, Pettigrew also encouraged the use of Sioux Falls quartzite in the construction of public buildings and secured appropriations from the federal government for that purpose. On September 8, 1891, Pettigrew wrote to the commissioner of Indian Affairs in Washington, D.C., regarding the establishment of an Indian School at Flandreau, South Dakota. Pettigrew had been instrumental in securing an appropriation of $50,000 with which to build the school (on land purchased from Pettigrew). Pettigrew wanted the school to be built of Sioux Falls quartzite. According to an article in the Flandreau *Herald* of January 1, 1892, he was successful in getting this specification inserted in the architect's plans and in the advertisement for bids from construction contractors.

Also early in his senatorial career, Pettigrew secured an appropriation of $150,000 from the federal government for the construction of a United States court house and post office in Sioux Falls. The building was to be built of Sioux Falls quartzite. The Hubbard Stone and Construction Company of Sioux Falls was awarded the contract to construct the building, which was completed and ready for occupancy in May 1895.

Other prominent buildings in Sioux Falls constructed of quartzite at the height of the quarry industry were the Minnehaha County Court House, Carnegie Library, the

Queen Bee Mill, at the Falls of the Big Sioux River. Siouxland Heritage Museums, Sioux Falls, South Dakota.

of outstanding examples of buildings constructed of this fine stone, many of them the work of the Hubbard Company. One picture was of the Minnehaha County Court House, built entirely of dark purple jasper in 1891 at a total cost of $100,000. The building measured 126 by 132 feet and was probably "the best public building for the cost in this country." Also shown was the home of J. W. Tuthill, "one of the most expensive residences in Sioux Falls," constructed of pink jasper and wood.

The brochure also included illustrations of jasper structures located in cities besides Sioux Falls: Ladies' Hall at the University of South Dakota in Vermillion, of purple jasper trimmed in dark red jasper; the Wesleyan M.E. Church in Minneapolis, Minnesota; and the W. B. Mundie residence, of dark pink jasper, in Chicago. Mundie was an architect of some renown, and, noted the brochure, "when an architect of the well-known prominence and ability of Mr. Mundie selects jasper for his own

South Dakota State Penitentiary, the State School for the Deaf, the Childrens' Home, Central Fire Station, Old Main and East Hall at Augustana College, Jorden Hall and Martin Glidden Hall at Sioux Falls College, Washington High School, All Saints School, Lowell School, the Congregational and Episcopal churches, and several private homes.

In 1895 the Hubbard Stone and Construction Company published a handsome booklet, the purpose of which was to acquaint people with the superior qualities of Sioux Falls jasper or quartzite. Lavishly illustrated, the brochure contained pictures

Sioux Falls Stock Yards Company, ca. 1891. Siouxland Heritage Museums, Sioux Falls, South Dakota.

Post office in Sioux Falls, South Dakota. The third floor had been added when this photograph was taken, sometime after 1912. R. E. Kolbe Dakota Collection.

Minnehaha County Court House, Sioux Falls, South Dakota, shortly after it was completed. Siouxland Heritage Museums, Sioux Falls, South Dakota.

South Dakota State Penitentiary, Sioux Falls, South Dakota. View from inside the walls. R. E. Kolbe Dakota Collection.

Lutheran Normal School, photograph taken in 1910. Merged with Augustana College in 1918. R. E. Kolbe Dakota Collection.

residence in the city of Chicago it speaks volumes for Sioux Falls Jasper."

For a time, Sioux Falls quartzite was in demand as building and paving stone all over the nation. Chicago, Omaha, Kansas City, Indianapolis, and Burlington, Iowa—all were using quartzite for paving. The same cities boasted buildings constructed of quartzite, as did cities as far away as Tacoma and Detroit.

Architects, contractors, and businessmen from Chicago, New York, Boston, and Philadelphia came to the quarries to see quartzite for themselves and learn of its wonderful properties. The *Chicago Herald* on June 27, 1891, reported one such excursion of prominent individuals who came to inspect the quarries of the Dakota and Minnesota Stone Company, which were located in North Sioux Falls. A special railroad car was chartered and attached to a train of the Chicago, Rock Island and Pacific Railway. The inspection party was composed of individuals from Chicago, Pittsburgh, and several cities in Iowa.

The Star of Pipestone, Minnesota, on July 17, 1891, reproduced an article from the *American Contractor,* describing an excursion of eastern architects and other interested persons to Pipestone for the purpose of examining the quartzite quarries. Again, a special railroad car was chartered, a Pullman Palace Car. It was attached to a passenger train on the Rock Island Road leaving Chicago. The visitors had traveled over one thousand miles because of their interest in what was to them a new building stone, new because they had not heard of it, although the poet Longfellow had written of it in his poem *The Song of Hiawatha:*

> On the Mountains of the Prairie,
> On the great Red Pipestone Quarry,
> Gitche Manito, the mighty,
> He the Master of Life, descending,
> On the red crags of the quarry
> Stood erect, and called the nations
> Called the tribes of men together.

According to the *American Contractor* article, among the qualities making quartzite a superior building stone was its ability to withstand high temperatures. The finest granite would crumble when subjected to the heat of a conflagration, but after nine months of use, the quartzite blocks used to line a furnace showed no appreciable deterioration. Quartzite was also easily quarried, its cleavage was perfect, and its beauty was unsurpassed. In short, agreed the eastern architects, quartzite from the quarries they visited was "the finest and handsomest building stone" they had ever seen.

Not only were the architects agreed on quartzite's attractiveness, they also believed that it was especially suited for use in large and smoky cities because it was impervious to moisture and would not be discolored by dust, smoke, or acid. Even a strong substance like muriatic acid has no perceptible effect on quartzite. Washing by rains or with a water hose restores its original beauty and color. Transportation of the heavy stone would not present a problem, because several railroad lines connected the quarries with all eastern cities. Even when shipping costs were added, quartzite was comparable in cost to such building materials as brick because it would last longer and provide better service.

After their inspection tour, the party of architects repaired to the Calumet, a fine three-story hotel built of red and gray jasper and pipestone. There the party was treated to a banquet as fine as any that could be obtained in the best eastern eating establishments. The menu included such delicacies as salmon, roast bear, pickled lamb's tongue, and shrimp salad—washed down with coffee, tea, and champagne. For dessert, guests could choose from eight varieties of cake, three flavors of ice cream, and an assortment of fruit.

Impressed with the quarries and the qualities of the stone they contained and struck by the surroundings and the friendliness of the people of Pipestone, the visitors, concluded the article, "will all henceforth be boomers for Pipestone building and paving stone and eagerly await its general use by architects, builders, and capitalists."

These architects were not the only people upon whom quartzite made a favorable impression. Samples of Sioux Falls quartzite were displayed at the World's Columbian Exposition in Chicago in 1893 where, according to the *Diamond Jubilee History of Jasper* (1963), it received the Exposition's First Award.

Notwithstanding the praises being sung to quartzite and its properties and the authority granted the secretary of the interior by senate bill 3089 to survey and mark the seventh standard parallel between the states of North and South Dakota, the secretary wanted to assure himself on a number of issues before allowing work to begin on the project. On December 3, 1890, he wrote to Commissioner Lewis A. Groff of the General Land Office asking him to

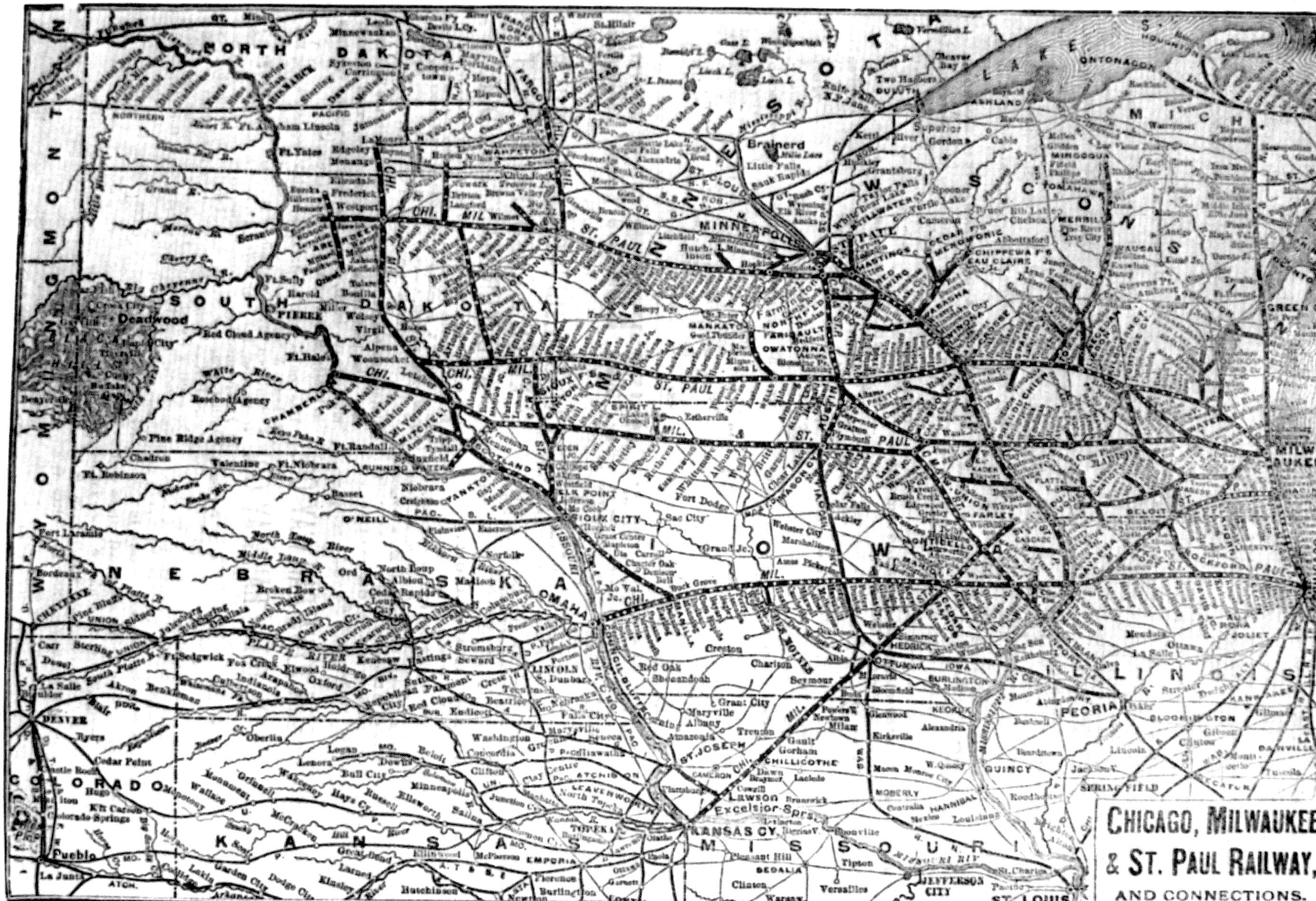

The routes of the Chicago, Milwaukee & St. Paul Railway, on which boundary monuments were shipped to White Rock, Newark, Frederick, and Eureka, South Dakota. Travelers' Official Railway Guide, *October 1892.*

make an estimate as soon as possible of how much the project would cost, to make a final determination of which quarries could furnish the stone for the monuments, and also to take the preliminary steps necessary for inviting bids for the survey and marking project.

Two months later, on January 31, 1891, Groff submitted his report. Groff had, upon the recommendation of Senator Pettigrew, determined to use a variety of quartzite for the monuments, a variety that was available in almost unlimited quantities from quarries in Sioux Falls. In a letter to Groff dated September 29, 1890, Pettigrew estimated that monuments five to six feet in length and eight to ten inches square could be obtained for five dollars each or less at the quarries. Pettigrew had also promised to provide an estimate of the cost of transporting the monuments to the boundary, but this he had neglected to do.

Groff had no means by which to make a fair estimate of the transportation costs, but he thought it safe to assume that the average cost to deliver each monument to its designated place on the boundary would be about ten dollars. The Chicago, Milwaukee & St. Paul Railway provided direct links with the boundary at three points east of the Missouri River – at White Rock, Newark, and north of Frederick, all towns in South Dakota. The same line provided freight service to Eureka, South Dakota, a town lying a few miles south of the state boundary. The monuments to be used west of the Missouri River could be shipped by rail to Pierre, South Dakota, and thence by steamboat to the boundary.

From the points reached by railroad and steamboat, the monuments would have to be transported by teams and wagons to the points along the boundary where each would be set. Transportation costs, especially west of the river, would be high. Nevertheless, estimated Groff, the total cost of each monument, including the initial cost, would be no more than about fifteen dollars.

Groff estimated that a total of 714 monuments would be required, making the total cost for the monuments $10,710. Congress had appropriated $25,000 for the project, so the amount available to pay for surveying the boundary would be $14,290, an amount equivalent to almost forty dollars per mile. Boundaries were customarily established at rates less than that, so Groff concluded that the $25,000 appropriation was sufficient. In fact, he thought it entirely possible that a competent surveyor could be found who would do the work for considerably less than the amount appropriated.

Although Groff did not think it likely that any surveying work could be done on the Dakota boundary before the middle of April or the first of May, he began immediately to prepare the bidding instructions and the contract specifications.

Preliminary work having been done and estimates obtained, Commissioner Groff, under the date of March 11, 1891, "in conformity with the act of September 25, 1890 and departmental instructions," inserted advertisements for "Proposals for Boundary Survey and Monuments" in newspapers published at Bismarck, North Dakota, and Huron, South Dakota. The advertisement appeared daily in the Bismarck *Daily Tribune,* except Sundays, between March 17, 1891, and April 12, 1891. The advertisement announced that:

> Sealed proposals will be received at the General Land Office, Washington, D.C., until 2 o'clock p.m., on Wednesday, the 15th day of April, 1891, for the survey of the boundary line between the states of North and South Dakota, and for the furnishing of stone monuments to be placed at half-mile intervals on said boundary. The bids for the survey and for the monuments must be separate, with the privilege to the bidder that if he is not awarded the contract for both, he will be bound to contract for neither. Copies of the specifications and general instructions may be had upon application to this office. Each bid must be accompanied by a certified check for $500. The right to reject any or all bids is reserved. Proposals must be inclosed in envelopes sealed and marked "Proposals for survey of boundary between North and South Dakota," and "Proposal for boundary monuments," and addressed to the Commissioner of the General Land Office, Washington, D.C.

By the time the advertisement was published, surveyors had less than one month in which to obtain the specifications from Washington, make a study of the project, calculate their costs, and submit their bids to the General Land Office. It was on March 20, 1891, that Charles H. Bates, the surveyor who was eventually awarded the surveying and marking contract, sent his request to the General Land Office for the specifications and bidding instructions.

On March 24, 1891, over the signature of acting commissioner William M. Stone, the General Land Office issued the specifications for the "Survey and marking of the Boundary line between North and South Dakota." The specifications dealing with the survey itself were surprisingly brief. The survey had to be done "in strict conformity with the laws of the United States, the printed manual of surveying instructions approved December 2, 1889, and other surveying instructions issued by the Commissioner of the General Land Office. . . . " The surveyor had to use "a first class Transit (by a reputable maker), and an accurate solar attachment of approved construction. . . . " The "Solar" could not be allowed to interfere with the use of the instrument as a *"transit."* Bidders for the survey were requested to enclose with their bid a full and detailed description of the instrument they proposed to use as well as the name of the manufacturer. The entire boundary had to be measured by two sets of chainmen working independently of each other.

The specifications for marking the boundary were as lengthy—twelve pages including diagrams—as those for the survey of the boundary were brief. According to the specifications, the boundary was to be "defined and perpetuated" by stone monuments located at intervals of one-half mile, beginning at or near the initial point and ending with the terminal monument on the Montana border.

Monuments were to be of "fine grain quartzite," which could be obtained at the quarries in Sioux Falls, South Dakota, and at other locations. The cost of marking the monuments and transporting them from the quarry to the line had to be included in the bids. Monuments had to be a minimum of seven feet long and ten inches square. They were to be placed in "a truly vertical position, set 3½ feet in the ground, and with their faces directed to the cardinal points." All monuments had to be "conspicuously, neatly and durably" marked with letters and figures *"cut,* clean and smooth," into the stone.

The size, position, and arrangement of all letters and figures had to conform to the specifications, a copy of which was sent to each prospective bidder. The wording and diagrams of the specifications are reproduced below, just as they were given in the original:

> All letters and figures (except fractions), are to be 2½ inches high, of proportionate width, and of the style known as "Egyptian;" they are to be

A transit, with solar attachment. Philip Kissam, Surveying for Civil Engineers, *© 1956, p. 239. Reproduced with permission by McGraw-Hill Book Company, Inc.*

perfectly plain. The groove or cut for the body of letters or figures 2½ ins. high, to be of triangular cross section (V shaped) 3-8 inches wide on face of stone, and ¼ inch deep. The cut for small figures (or letters), ¼ inch wide and 1-8 in. deep. . . .

The upper line of the highest letter or figure, on any face, to be 6 inches from top of post. A blank space, 2½ inches wide, to be left between consecutive lines. All posts are to be left rough, as they come from the quarry, except where markings are required, and for these, the stone must be dressed to a proper surface to receive the letters and figures required, as follows:

1. On the *east* side of every ½ mile post the fraction "½" (figures 1¼ inches high), and following the same the letter "M", size and arrangement as shown on diagram No. 1.

2. On the *east* side of all mile posts, the letter "M", and above it the number of miles from the initial monument. (See diagram No. 2.)

3. All posts, both mile and ½ mile, are to have, on the *north* side, the letters "N.D." and on the *south* side the letters "S.D." (See diagram No. 3.)

4. Across the S. and W. [Sisseton and Wahpeton] Indian Reservation and west of the Missouri River, in addition to marks above specified, every sixth mile post or standard township corner – counting from the 1st S. Tp. corner – is to be marked on its *north* face "S.C." 6 ins. below "N.D." and "T. 129," 2½ ins. below "S.C." The same posts are to be marked, at an equal distance from top, and on the E. and W. faces, with an "R" and the range number, 2½ ins. below it. (See diagram No. 4.)

5. The intermediate mile posts – standard section corners – are to be marked on their north faces with letters "S.C." 6 ins. below "N.D." and with grooves on their *east* and *west* sides to correspond in number to the distance in miles to the nearest standard township corner which they face. The *grooves* are to be of the width and depth prescribed for the large letters, and 2½ ins. long, placed horizontally 1 inch apart, 6 inches below the other markings. (See diagram No. 5.)

6. The ½ mile posts are to be marked "$\frac{1/4}{\text{S.C.}}$" on their north face, 6 ins. below the letters "N.D." (See diagram No. 6.)

Detailed directions for marking the *Initial* and *Terminal* Monuments will be given in special instructions. All missing, or imperfectly marked old standard corners, are to be re-established in their original position, and the monuments marked as prescribed for the new surveys.

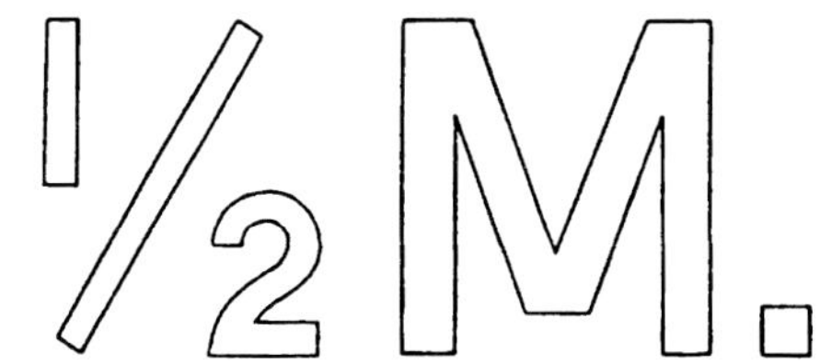

DIAGRAM NO. 1
Mark for east *face of all ½ mile monuments*

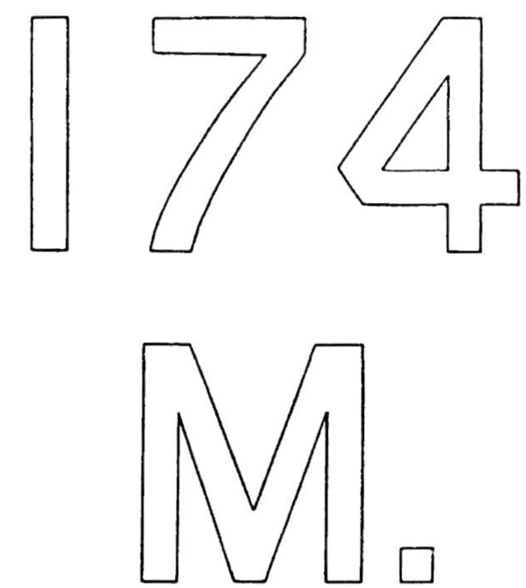

DIAGRAM NO. 2
The upper *mark for* east *face of 174th* mile *post.*

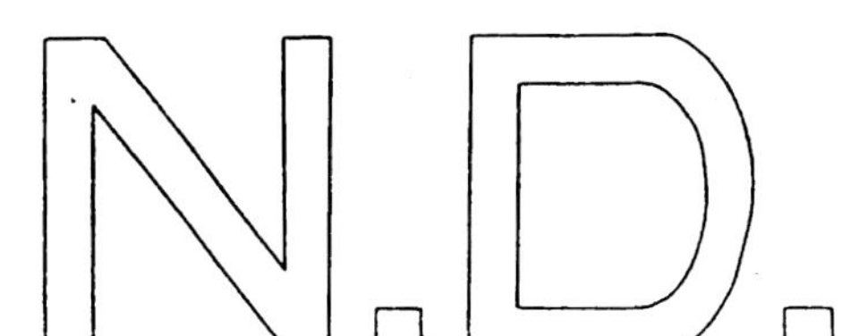

DIAGRAM NO. 3
The upper *mark for* north *face of all ½ mile and* mile *posts.*

DIAGRAM NO. 4 (Part 1)
The lower *marking for* north *face of Standard Township Corners through S. and W. Indian Reservation and* west *of Missouri River. For corresponding marks on East and West faces of same posts, See Part 2.*

DIAGRAM NO. 4 (Part 2)
The lower *marking for* east *face of Standard Township Corners through S. and W. Indian Reservation and west of Missouri River. The corresponding mark for* west *face of same post will be obtained by changing "84" to "85."*

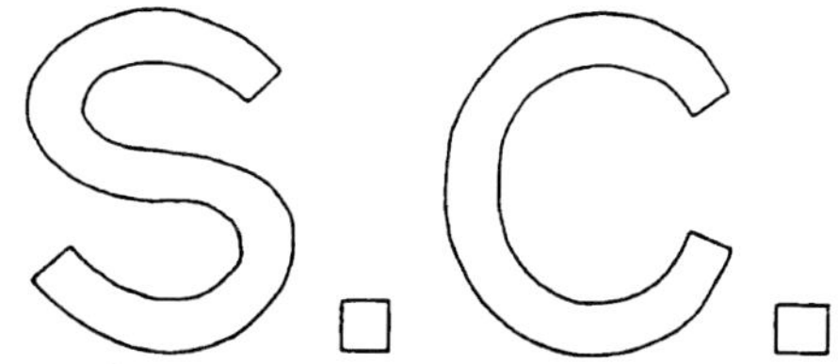

DIAGRAM NO. 5 (Part 1)
The lower *marks for north face of* mile *posts or Standard* Section *Corners, through S. and W. Indian Reservation and west of Missouri River. For corresponding mark on east and west faces, see Part 2.*

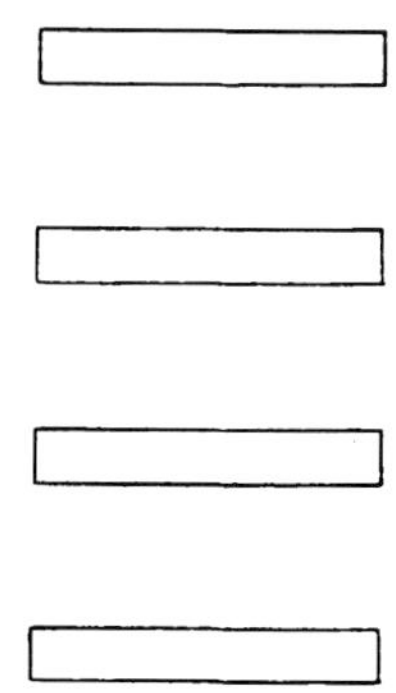

DIAGRAM NO. 5 (Part 2)
The lower *marks* on east *face of post at corner for sections 32 and 33, supposed to be a Standard* Sec*tion Corner. The corresponding marks on west side of same post will be of similar form with 2 grooves instead of 4. To be placed on Standard Section Corners within the S. and W. Indian Reservation and on those west of the Missouri River.*

DIAGRAM NO. 6
The lower *mark for* north *side of all ½ mile posts (Standard ¼ Section Corners), through S. and W. Indian Reservation and* west *of the Missouri River.*

The deadline for submitting bids for surveying and marking the North and South Dakota boundary was April 15, 1891. Three weeks later, on May 8, Thomas H. Carter, formerly United States Representative from Montana and newly appointed commissioner of the General Land Office, informed the secretary of the interior by letter that a total of five bids had been received by the deadline.

C. W. Hubbard of Sioux Falls, South Dakota, agreed to survey the boundary and furnish the monuments for $21,500. Written in the margin of Carter's letter of transmittal was the notation that, although Hubbard was not a surveyor, he had been recommended by Pettigrew. After the receipt of Hubbard's bid, however, and before the contracts were awarded, the Sioux Falls Granite Company, of which

Hubbard was general manager, was placed in receivership. The Sioux Falls *Daily Argus Leader* in its issue of April 25, 1891, stated that the company had been in financial difficulties for some time and that a large number of its paving blocks had been rejected by some eastern contractors. The same information was added in longhand in the margin of Carter's letter to the secretary of the interior.

Charles H. Bates, of Yankton, South Dakota, offered to survey and mark the boundary for $17,000. He would furnish the stone monuments on board the cars in Jasper or North Sioux Falls—the freight rates were the same from both points—for $4,300, making a total bid for the project of $21,300.

F. W. Pettigrew of Sioux Falls, South Dakota, the senator's brother and an experienced surveyor, offered to survey and mark the boundary for $17,500. Contrary to instructions, he did not submit a bid for furnishing the stone monuments.

George E. Sherry and Company of Rochester, New York, was willing to survey and mark the boundary for $13,979 and would furnish the stone monuments on board the cars at St. Cloud, Minnesota, for an additional $3,000.45. The total of the Sherry bid was $16,979.45, the lowest and most detailed bid submitted.

Chalmers Curtis *et al.* of Webster, South Dakota, offered to survey and mark the line for $17,000. If the company was required to furnish the monuments, the total bid would be $22,000.

In his letter of May 8, 1891, to the secretary of the interior, Carter noted that the bids submitted by Bates and George E. Sherry and Company were the lowest received. In determining which of the bids to recommend accepting, Carter had used two criteria: first, the professional standing and reputation of the bidder, and, second, the quality of stone to be used for the monuments. Bates, wrote Carter, "has been long and favorably known to this office, and his reputation as a competent and reliable deputy surveyor is excelled by none." Bates had been awarded many contracts to run government surveys in Dakota Territory and he had invariably done good work. Moreover, the stone he proposed to use for the monuments was the "fine grain" Sioux Falls quartzite that had been referred to in the specifications.

Of the George E. Sherry Company, its reputation, and its surveying skills, on the other hand, the General Land Office possessed no information whatsoever. Nor did the General Land Office have any information about the quarries in Minnesota from which the company proposed to obtain the stone for the monuments.

The Sherry Company's bid was about $4,300 less than that of Bates', but, wrote Carter, "in view of [Bates'] well known professional skill and reputation, the certainty of his using for monuments stone of requisite quality and durability, as per specification, I am constrained to designate the bid of Mr. Bates as the proper one to accept, bearing in mind the necessity of having the work executed in a thorough and satisfactory manner."

In the advertisement inviting bids, the General Land Office had reserved the right to reject any and all submitted. Accordingly, Carter asked that his office be authorized to enter into a contract with Bates for surveying and marking the boundary between North and South Dakota even though his bid had not been the lowest. Carter also recommended that the contract for running the survey and furnishing and erecting the monuments be awarded *"to one and the same party."* Any division of work, for example, awarding the survey contract to one bidder and the monument contract to another, might hinder the beginning of the survey and delay its completion. By May, the surveying season was already well advanced, and Carter wanted the contract to be awarded as quickly as possible so that the successful bidder could begin his work immediately.

The news that Bates had been awarded the contract to survey and mark the boundary was carried by newspapers all across the state of South Dakota during the first days of May 1891. When Pettigrew learned of the General Land Office's choice, he was almost beside himself with anger and frustration. Pettigrew had not favored Bates and had not recommended him.

The boundary had attracted a great deal of attention. Many individuals had written to Pettigrew asking to be recommended for the surveying contract. On September 20, 1890, Pettigrew had written to a Thomas A. Bones of Hot Springs, South Dakota, in response to one such request. Pettigrew denied having anyone in mind to recommend for the contract, but he noted that because the project involved a state boundary, it would require expensive equipment, such as a theodolite, and also skills that not every surveyor possessed. An E. Huntington of Webster, South Dakota, had also asked for Pettigrew's recommendation. In his reply to Huntington on September 29,

1890, Pettigrew again denied having anyone in mind for the contract. It was his opinion, however, that the contract should be let to a skilled engineer or surveyor and he noted that Huntington was neither.

But Pettigrew did have someone in mind to survey and mark the boundary. His choice was C. W. Hubbard. Hubbard was neither a surveyor nor an engineer, and Pettigrew had put off other petitioners by stressing that the project required extraordinary engineering and surveying skills. Nevertheless, in a letter to Commissioner Carter at the General Land Office, on May 1, 1891, Pettigrew stressed that the engineering aspects of the project were not as important as those involving the monuments. In fact, wrote Pettigrew, the engineering aspects were "exceedingly simple" and could be done by anyone who knew how to run a solar compass.

Hubbard was not an engineer, admitted Pettigrew, but he was associated with as good an engineer as could be found in South Dakota, he was a contractor—he had the contract for the United States court house and post office in Sioux Falls—and he knew the Sioux Falls stone industry. Pettigrew asked Carter to award Hubbard the contract to survey and mark the boundary if his bid was the lowest and, vowed the senator, "I will guarantee that the work done by him will be first class in every particular."

Bates' bid was lower than Hubbard's by only $200, and Pettigrew was convinced that Bates' bid had been altered after it had arrived in Washington in order to make it more attractive and more competitive. Pettigrew frequently corresponded with Smith D. Fry, a newspaper correspondent, apparently free-lance, in Washington, D.C., who represented himself as a "Capital Reporter." The senator described Fry as "a bright and active man . . . " and frequently relied on him for information.

On May 19, 1891, Pettigrew wrote to Fry of his conviction that Hubbard's bid had originally been lower than the one submitted by Bates and that Bates' bid had been changed by one Joe Bailey. "Joe Bailey," charged Pettigrew, "is an unscrupulous scoundrel, and I don't intend to allow him to interfere and meddle with matters any further in Washington." Once the Senate was again in session, Pettigrew intended to pursue with that body the possibility that Bates' bid had been altered, but in the meantime he wanted Fry to learn what he could about the process by which the bids had been accepted and the contract awarded.

Bates' bid could stand on its merits, and it may have been no more than pique that caused Pettigrew to persist in his accusations that Bates had gotten the contract by underhanded means. Nevertheless, the senator would hold Bates accountable, and there was a means at hand. The survey and marking project had to be checked for accuracy before the federal government would accept it, pay Bates for his work, and release him from his oath and bond. George G. Beardsley, a surveyor from McCanna, North Dakota, secured the contract to check Bates' work.

North Sioux Falls Quarry. Pipestone County Historical Society.

On September 3, 1891, Pettigrew wrote to Beardsley and asked him to perform his inspection duties diligently, because, wrote the senator, the contract to survey and mark the boundary "was obtained by Bates and Joe Bailey and I want to compel them to fulfill the job according to specifications in every detail. I don't care if they lose some money. They secured it by underhanded means and by trickery and fraud and now I want them to fulfill it according to the letter. We will thus have a first class job."

Awarding the contracts for surveying and marking the boundary to Bates meant that Sioux Falls quartzite would be the stone used for the monuments. According to articles in the Jasper *Journal* and the Sioux Falls *Daily Argus Leader* early in May 1891, the contract for supplying the monuments was awarded to the North Sioux Falls Stone Company, whose business address was 307-308 in the Mulhall block. According to the Sioux Falls city directories, the North Sioux Falls Stone Company was in business from 1891 to 1895, possibly until 1896. The company may not have owned any quarries and may have been only a dealer in stone. In addition to furnishing the stone for the boundary monuments, the company seems also to have furnished some of the material for the Minnehaha County court house, which was being constructed at the same time that the boundary was being surveyed and marked. Thomas Bell McMartin, one of the city's most prominent and successful lawyers, was president of the North Sioux Falls Stone Company. His fine home, an 1889 Queen Anne, was constructed from quartzite and brick. Former Senator Pettigrew purchased the home in May 1911. It is today the Pettigrew Museum.

Bates was notified on May 9, 1891, by Commissioner Carter of the General Land Office that he had been awarded the contract for running the boundary line between the two Dakotas. Because the surveying season in the latitude of the seventh standard parallel was short and already well advanced, Bates waited impatiently for Washington to supply him with the contract, the forms for his oath and bond, and the special instructions pertaining to his carrying out the terms of the contract. Not until May 23, and only after Bates had again requested the necessary forms, did William M. Stone, the acting commissioner of the General Land Office, send them. Stone informed Bates that the special instructions, for example, those pertaining to the initial

The Thomas Bell McMartin residence, 131 North Duluth, Sioux Falls, South Dakota. Now the Pettigrew Museum. Siouxland Heritage Museums, Sioux Falls, South Dakota.

and terminal monuments, had not yet been prepared.

On June 4, 1891, Bates signed Contract Number 56269, an agreement between himself and the United States government. By the terms of the contract, Bates agreed that he,

> with the assistance of such chainmen, axmen, flagbearers, and others, as may be necessary, in strict conformity with the laws of the United States, the printed manual of surveying instructions approved December 2, 1889, and other surveying instructions issued by the Commissioner of the General Land Office, and with such special instructions as he may receive from the said Commissioner in conformity therewith (all of said instructions being hereby incorporated with and made a part of this contract), will well, truly, and faithfully survey, mark, and establish by suitable and permanent monuments, the Seventh Standard Parallel of public land surveys, between the States of North Dakota and South Dakota from the Bois des Sioux River to the twenty-seventh degree of West Longitude from Washington (as surveyed and established for the Boundary between the Territories of Dakota and Montana by Daniel G. Major under contract with the Commissioner of the General Land Office dated June 20, 1885), and that he will complete these surveys in the manner aforesaid, and return the true field-notes thereof in triplicate and plats in triplicate, to the office of the said Commissioner on or before the first day of November, 1892, on penalty of forfeiture, and paying to the United States the sum of forty-two thousand six hundred dollars, lawful money of the United States (being double the estimated amount which would be due by the United States to the said Charles H. Bates upon the completion of the surveys named in this contract), if default be made in any of the fore going conditions.

The contract provided that Bates could receive partial payment (ninety percent) for completing that portion of the survey east of the Missouri River before completing the survey west of the river. The final payment would be made when the entire boundary had been surveyed, but the sum of all payments could not exceed $21,300. Bates was also specifically prohibited from allowing any other surveyor or contractor to perform any of the work for which he was being paid.

On June 8, 1891, Bates wrote to Carter and enclosed the signed contract; his oath, which he had signed June 6; and his bond, which was dated June 4. Porter P. Peck of Sioux Falls and Sanford B. Carlson of Yankton had signed affidavits of sureties in the amount of $42,600 on Bates' behalf. Bates asked Carter to return to the Minnehaha National Bank in Sioux Falls the two certified checks for $500 each that he had included when he had submitted his bids for the survey of the boundary and for furnishing the monuments.

Thomas H. Carter signed the contract on behalf of the United States government on June 15, 1891, and it, together with Bates' bond, was approved by the acting secretary of the interior on July 20, 1891. The legalities had been taken care of and Bates had received his general instructions. Bates could not get into the field and begin surveying the boundary, however, until he had received the necessary special instructions which had been promised him and for which he now began an impatient wait.

Chapter 5

From the Initial Monument to Monument 190

"Silent sentinels on the prairie. . . . "
Charles H. Bates

Charles H. Bates, the man to whom the contract was awarded to survey and mark the boundary between North and South Dakota, occupies a unique if little known place in the history of the Dakotas, possibly in the history of the nation. He alone, of all surveyors of the public domain, marked a long state boundary with magnificent stone monuments placed every one-half mile along its entire length.

Described as "an old settler and one of the best known men in South Dakota" in the 1897 edition of the South Dakota *Compendium of Biography,* Bates was born in Milan, Ohio, on April 12, 1850, the son of Evelyn Bates, a native of Connecticut. Evelyn Bates was a shipbuilder, and from him Charles learned the carpenter's trade.

After completing his education and after working as a carpenter for two years, Charles Bates moved west. He reached Yankton, Dakota Territory, in 1869 and was engaged as an assistant in the service of the United States land survey under Moses K. Armstrong. He was soon appointed deputy United States land surveyor, and after 1870 he was engaged in surveying the public lands on both sides of the Missouri River in what became North and South Dakota. Senator Pettigrew in early 1891 described Bates as "one of the best workmen in the state" and recommended that the General Land Office pay him for having completed a surveying contract, "without the formality of an inspection," which Pettigrew believed was "wholly unnecessary."

Charles H. Bates, United States Surveyor who established the North Dakota-South Dakota boundary. Yankton County Museum, Yankton, South Dakota.

In 1876 Bates married Julia Ash, the daughter of Henry Clay and Mary Ash. Ash was born in Allegheny County, Maryland, on December 25, 1827, and was raised in Indiana. Kingsbury in his *History of Dakota Territory* described him as "a whole souled, genial Hoosier, and possibly the most popular of all the early pioneers . . . " in Dakota.

Ash and his wife came to Yankton from Sioux City and opened the Ash Hotel on Christmas Day 1859. Mrs. Ash, known through the country as "Mother Ash," was the first white woman to live in Yankton. Their daughter Lizzie was the first white child born in Dakota Territory. Henry Clay Ash was a member of the territorial legislature for two terms and was the United States deputy marshal in Yankton

Mr. and Mrs. Henry Clay Ash, proprietors of the first hotel in Yankton and Charles H. Bates' in-laws. George W. Kingsbury, A History of Dakota Territory.

before he moved to Deadwood in 1877. In 1878 he moved to Sturgis, where he was the city's first justice of the peace. He also engaged in farming.

Bates, in addition to being a surveyor, ran a hardware store in Yankton from 1879 to 1881. From 1888 to 1889, he was in the grocery business. He was city engineer one term, city marshal one term, member of the city council one term, and city and school treasurer two terms.

The great flood in the spring of 1881 inundated the wide bottom lands of the Missouri River between Yankton and the Sioux River. Yankton sustained heavy damage; Vermillion was almost completely destroyed; and Meckling, a railroad station on the Dakota Southern railroad about seven miles west of Vermillion, was isolated and its inhabitants in danger for their lives. Bates and other courageous men from Yankton braved the flood and made many attempts to reach the marooned people by boats, but they were repeatedly turned back by barriers of ice and raging water.

Bates also served many years as an alloting agent for Indians in southwestern South Dakota. Batesland, a small Shannon County town on the edge of the Pine Ridge Indian Reservation, described by the *South Dakota Guide* as a group of buildings huddled together for mutual protection on the prairie hinterland, is named for him.

In 1891, when Bates undertook to survey and mark the boundary between North and South Dakota, he had more than twenty years' experience with Dakota weather. He had always counted on being able to work in the field until Christmas and made his calculations accordingly.

The 1887 edition of *Resources of Dakota* described autumn as "a delightful season" in Dakota, with good weather lasting far into December. Extremely cold and unpleasant weather usually did not occur until after the holidays. Fort Yates on the Missouri River, the nearest reporting point to where Bates would be when he finished work on the boundary for the season, enjoyed a mean November temperature of 28.6°F. Records were available only since 1882, but in Bismarck—the next closest reporting point—one could expect November to have ten clear days, fourteen fair days, and six cloudy days.

Although the statistics suggested good weather to the end of 1891, as in previous years, Bates was skeptical. Eastern weather forecasters were unanimous in predicting that severe weather would arrive a month earlier than usual in 1891, and, as Bates reported to the Yankton *Press and Dakotan* in November 1891 at the close of the surveying season, they were right.

By May 9, when Bates was notified by Commissioner Carter of the General Land Office that he had been awarded the contract for running and marking the boundary, the surveying season was already well advanced. Bates was eager to get into the field, and he was impatient with Washington for failing to send him the instructions and specifications that he needed before beginning work. Major papers, such as the Yankton *Press and Dakotan* and the Sioux Falls *Daily Argus Leader,* reported in

May that Bates hoped to be in the field in July, but not even at that late date could Bates begin the survey.

On June 8, when Bates mailed his contract, bond, and oath to the General Land Office, his impatience and frustration were revealed with his request that, if complete instructions regarding the survey and plats were not yet available, could he at least receive "*immediate* information" on one specific question. The first section corner on the boundary was 51.00 chains west from the Bois des Sioux River. Would the monument placed in this corner be marked "mile post No. l" and from that corner would the monuments be marked in sequence to the Missouri River? An "immediate answer" was required, insisted Bates, so that workmen at the quarry could proceed with the marking of the monuments. Bates was having the markings placed on the monuments by experienced stone cutters at the quarry—at "a large additional expense"—rather than having the markings placed on the monuments by novices as they were set. The neatness and quality of workmanship justified the additional expense.

A week later, on June 13, Carter complied with Bates' request by sending the following instructions:

> The monument to be placed at the standard corner for sections 33 and 34, of township 129 north, range 47 west 5th P.M. which is reported to be 51 chs., west of the west bank of the Bois des Sioux River, is to be marked for and called the *first* mile post, and thence the monuments at the consecutive standard section and township corners on the 7th standard parallel (as established or to be established), are to be marked in a continuous series, as the 2nd, 3rd, 4th, etc., mile posts, to the east boundary of Montana, and the 1/2 mile posts are to be set at the intermediate standard 1/4 section corners.

The inscription for the initial monument and its location could not be determined until Bates had retraced that part of the seventh standard parallel immediately west of the Bois des Sioux River. Those instructions, wrote Carter, would be included with Bates' special instructions, which would be sent to him in a few days.

By July 22 Bates had not yet received his special instructions, and on that date he sent a telegram, from Sturgis where he was working, to Carter at the General Land Office asking, "when will boundary instructions be mailed [?] Please wire information immediately." By telegram the next day, Carter informed Bates that the special instructions had been prepared. They were sent under cover of a letter from Carter dated July 25, 1891.

Carter reminded Bates that he would be governed in running the survey by the terms of his contract; by the *Manual of Surveying Instructions,* approved December 2, 1889; by the "Specification of the survey and marking" (a copy of which he already had); as well as by the detailed set of special instructions, for which he had been waiting.

Bates was to begin his survey at the standard corner for sections 31 and 32, township 129 north, range 54 west of the fifth principal meridian system, that is, a short distance west of the Sisseton and Wahpeton Indian Reservation. After identifying and verifying the position of this corner, he was to make careful observations on Polaris, at elongation, to determine the true meridian and then lay off an angle of ninety degrees to the east and prolong this direction in a straight line (tangent to the parallel of latitude) by double backsights and foresights at each setting of his instrument, a convenient distance not exceeding twelve miles.

These instructions were subsequently changed, on July 28, and Bates was authorized to use tables I and II of the *Manual of Surveying Instructions* in his retracements east of the Missouri River, rather than observations of elongations of Polaris. Bates could use his solar, which had to be in perfect adjustment, to verify the direction of his tangent lines. Bates was also to make whatever measurements were necessary to re-establish missing standard quarter, section, and township corners in their original positions.

The "Initial Point" of the boundary would be that point where the seventh standard parallel intersected with the main channel of the Bois des Sioux River. The initial monument could not be placed at the initial point, that is in the channel of the river, so it was to be placed due west from the initial point "upon the nearest solid ground favorable for its proper and convenient establishment and suitable for its protection and preservation."

If the "Initial Monument" were to be marked with its initials only (I.M.), they might be understood to stand for "one mile." Bates was, therefore, to mark the east face of the monument with the abbreviations "In. Mt.," placed horizontally six inches below the top. Starting three inches below that mark were to be placed letters and figures to read down the monument as follows: "In. Pt. 18 C.E." for "Initial Point 18 Chains East." In place of "18," he was to insert the actual distance to the initial point.

The north and south faces of the initial monument would bear the letters N.D. and S.D., as would all other monuments. On the west face, the date 1891 was to be placed across the monument six inches from the top. Below the date,the monument was to be faced to receive, at some future time when it had been determined, the correct latitude. (The figure for the correct latitude has never been placed on the initial monument.)

No half-mile monument would be required between the river and the first mile monument, which would be placed at the standard corner for sections 33 and 34. Thence the monuments were to be placed at the standard section and township corners on the seventh standard parallel and were to be marked in a continuous series to the east boundary of Montana. The half-mile monuments were to be set at the intermediate standard quarter section corners.

Admonished by Carter to take "great care" in order to avoid mistakes, Bates was instructed to:

> give in your field notes full and complete records of your observations for true meridians, give the true course and length of each 1/2 mile of the line, and fully note the topography of the country 1/4 of a mile on each side of the line, where practicable. Houses and all other important artificial objects, as well as natural features, should be accurately located by intersecting bearings from standard corners or other known points.

As was customary, Bates' field notes had to contain complete records of all observations and the direction and length of all offsets from the tangent to the parallel. When he crossed the Missouri River, Bates was to use at least two independent, well-conditioned triangles by which to determine the width of the river. Computations and illustrative diagrams were to be inserted in the field notes. Field notes had to be neatly and legibly written on official field note paper and fastened or bound on the long side. Finally, Bates was requested to keep the General Land Office informed of his post office address so that communications from Washington could reach him.

Seven sets of field notes, recording earlier surveys relating to the seventh standard parallel, were sent to Bates to aid him in his task of locating and retracing the parallel between the Bois des Sioux and Missouri rivers. Supplemental instructions would be sent later for running the survey west of the Missouri River.

Bates noted in a letter to Carter on August 21 that following the *Manual of Surveying Instructions* would present problems. For example, building mounds two to three feet high at each standard corner would cover up most of the lettering on the monuments. Why not, asked Bates, modify the instructions and allow the monument to constitute the corner, rather than using pits and mounds? Bates had also been studying the field notes that had been sent to him and he anticipated difficulty locating nearly obliterated corners and meander corners, especially near the Missouri River, because field notes and diagrams were not in agreement in their descriptions of the topography nor on the amount of timber and brush along the parallel. Bates also informed Carter that because he had waited so long for his instructions he would be unable to do anything on the boundary west of the Missouri River during the 1891 season.

Carter mailed Bates' final instructions to his Sturgis address on August 31, 1891. Because of "the large size, permanent and durable character of the monuments and the complete marking" on them for standard corners, wrote Carter, Bates would not have to construct pits and mounds.

Where stones or posts marking standard corners were found, they were to be taken up and the monument "planted in its exact place, the vertical axes marking the corner." (There are forty chains in a half mile and eighty chains in a full mile. On much of the boundary between Minnesota and the Missouri River, however, Bates was retracing a survey in which slight errors had been made in the location of some standard corners. They were not always exactly forty or eighty chains apart. Bates could only verify the original corners, mark them with monuments, and record the actual distances between them in his field notes.) The old stone or post was to be placed on and against the north side of the monument so that its marks, if any, could be read. Only enough earth was to be placed around the monument to allow for settling, and it should be sodded where there was grass.

Surplus earth from the hole for the monument was to be placed in a pile with its center four feet north of the corner.

With the receipt of his final instructions, Bates could begin the work of surveying and marking the seventh standard parallel between North and South Dakota. Informed in early May that he had received the contract, he had been seriously delayed by the lack of instructions, and it was September before he could set out for the boundary. He had perhaps three months, no more than four, remaining in the 1891 surveying season in which to retrace or survey 190 miles of the parallel and transport and erect about 380 monuments. Time was at a premium.

While waiting on Washington for the final instructions relating to surveying and marking the Dakota boundary, Bates was completing a surveying contract in the Black Hills and in the Badlands. On this contract, too, Bates met with delays. The Sturgis *Weekly Record* in its edition of August 21 noted Bates' vexation at having to run new lines because of "outrageous work [done] by a previous deputy surveyor. . . ." Bates' crew, however, was experiencing no difficulty finding water – a common problem experienced by surveyors when engaged in surveying the public domain, especially on the Great Plains – because more rain had fallen in the area in 1891 than in the previous ten years.

Indeed, crops were so good in Meade County because of the ample moisture that farmers were in despair. According to the Sturgis *Weekly Record* of August 28, a farmer had visited the newspaper's office with tears in his eyes, refusing to be comforted until he learned that his neighbors were experiencing the same problem he was. His grain crop was so bountiful that he did not have enough land on which to set his grain shocks after the grain had been cut. His only recourse was to rent a hay field on which to set some of the shocks. Even then, he would have no space on which to set the threshing machine when it came to his place.

Having completed his surveying in western South Dakota, Bates made ready to begin work on his contract to survey and mark the seventh standard parallel. In his field notes, he gave September 19, 1891, as the date for the commencement of the survey. On the previous day, September 18, Bates' assistants swore their preliminary oaths before him as United States deputy surveyor and as notary public. The crew consisted of G. W. Osborn and Fred O. LaFollette, chainmen; Elial W. Hinsdale and Charles Wright, chainmen and moundmen; Frank Wallace, G. W. Theim, and R. R. Cos, moundmen; and William Jones, flagman and moundman. The oath taken by the chainmen was:

> We [here follow the names] do solemnly swear that we will well and faithfully execute the duties of Chain Carriers; that we will level the Chain over even and uneven ground, and plumb the tally pins, either by sticking or dropping the same, that we will report the true lengths of all lines that we assist in measuring to the best of our skill and ability; . . .

The preliminary oath to which the moundmen swore was:

> We [here follow the names] do solemnly swear that we will well and truly perform the duties of moundsmen in the establishment of corners and other duties according to instructions given us. . . .

Fort Yates and Standing Rock Agency, taken from the northwest. South Dakota State Historical Society.

Site of Winona, North Dakota (1884-1915). The town was located near the ranch buildings above the center of the photograph. South Dakota State Historical Society.

Few bridges spanned the Missouri River in 1891; most crossings were made, therefore, by ferry. Leaving Sturgis, Bates and his men headed cross country towards Fort Yates, which was on the west bank of the Missouri River and a few miles north of the state boundary. A ferry plied the river between Fort Yates and Winona, North Dakota. As set by the Ferry Law in 1892, rates were one dollar for a team and loaded wagon and ten cents per one hundred pounds of freight or merchandise.

The town of Winona apparently sprang up in early 1884. A post office was established in May with James G. Pitts as postmaster. Later that year the town was surveyed and platted. The first permanent buildings were erected in September. Called the "Devil's Colony" and other uncomplimentary names, Winona early enjoyed a richly deserved unsavory reputation.

The town was outside the limits of the Standing Rock Reservation and outside the jurisdiction of the fort, so soldiers, Indians, traders, freighters, and cowboys came to town to enjoy the night life in the many saloons (as many as nine at one time) with their expansive bars and amiable hostesses. Winona also had an excellent racetrack where much money changed hands. Drunkenness was rampant and revelry often continued throughout the night. At times, timid residents felt themselves to be in danger for life and limb from stray bullets and drunken men and women.

In 1884, soon after the establishment of the town, the medical officer at Fort Yates complained that because of the ease with which whiskey could be obtained in the town there was a high incidence of brawling and desertions at the post. Drunken soldiers sometimes froze to death. The Indian agent at Standing Rock Agency complained that, with Winona so close, Indians could easily obtain liquor, especially during the winter when they could walk across the frozen river. They returned to the reservation, distributed whiskey to other Indians, and committed acts they would not have had they been sober. When North Dakota entered the Union in 1889 as a "dry" state, the saloons had to go under cover. They were now called "poolhalls," "dance halls," and "soft-drink parlors." Jack Flynn cheekily named his establishment "The Temperance Hall."

The birth of Linton and its designation as the seat of Emmons County spelled the end of Winona. Today, intoned the writers of the Emmons County history, "like Sodom and Gomorrah, its site . . . lies beneath the murky waters of the [Missouri] river."

Winona also had a good and law-abiding element and could boast of a newspaper, a Sunday School, a literary society, a dramatic club, a school, and several hotels and businesses. A boomer ad sponsored by the Missouri River Land and Improvement Company in the September 3, 1891, issue of the Winona *Times* drew attention to the town's attractions.

Winona was situated sixty miles downstream from Bismarck on the east bank of the Missouri River and was the best town between Bismarck and Pierre. The town was easily reached by stage and steamboat from Bismarck and points downriver. Winona's natural levee and steamboat landing fronting on the business street could be used at any stage of water, and, unusual for the Missouri River, the channel had not changed at Winona for the previous twelve years. Several freighting outfits were engaged in hauling grain and freight between Winona-Fort Yates and Bismarck, Eureka, and the Black Hills.

The land around Winona was magnificent prairie, well watered and

Winona Times *office and C. Patterson home. Winona school in the background.* Emmons County History.

beautifully timbered. The soil was unsurpassed anywhere in the world for raising livestock and crops. Winona presented tempting openings for all types of businesses because of its location on the river directly opposite from and connected by ferry with Fort Yates—a six-company post—and Standing Rock Indian Agency—which administered a reservation containing five thousand Indians.

If, when they passed through Winona, Bates and his men were suffering from lethargy, they could cleanse their systems with Syrup of Figs, advertised in the Winona *Times* and available locally. Refreshing to the taste, Syrup of Figs acted gently, yet promptly, on the kidneys, liver, and bowels to cleanse the system; dispel colds, headaches, and fevers; and cure chronic constipation. Or the men could fortify themselves for the task ahead of them, purify their blood, invigorate their livers, strengthen their nerves, and sharpen their appetites by drinking Hood's Sarsaparilla. Carter's Little Liver Pills were also available, and they were guaranteed to relieve the distress caused by dyspepsia, indigestion, or a torpid liver.

As reported by the official *Records from Fort Yates,* Winona sustained an outbreak of diphtheria during August 1891. When Dr. H. M. Deeble, the acting assistant surgeon at Fort Yates, returned from temporary duty at Fort Abraham Lincoln on August 21, he learned that a severe form of throat disease had broken out in Winona. Assisted by a Dr. Quinland of New York, a specialist on diseases of the throat who happened to be visiting at the post, Deeble investigated and confirmed that a number of townspeople were suffering from diphtheria. The post commander immediately issued an order prohibiting any intercourse between Fort Yates and the town of Winona. Guards were placed on the banks of the river to enforce the order, the ferry was closed, and all incoming mail was taken to the post hospital and fumigated before distribution. When no new cases of diphtheria were reported in Winona by the end of the month, Dr. Deeble fumigated the town, and the quarantine was lifted on September 6—shortly before Bates and the members of his survey party passed through.

Bates crossed the Missouri River at Fort Yates and proceeded south to the boundary between North and South Dakota. According to his field notes, he commenced the survey on September 19, 1891. The instruments Bates used were a Heller and Brightly transit with a Smith solar attachment made by Young and Sons. Both instruments had been adjusted to the meridian at the surveyor general's office at Huron. Chaining was done with two steel tapes adjusted to a length of sixty-six feet from a standard tape, which had also been adjusted at the surveyor general's office at Huron.

Having reached the seventh standard parallel at the corner for sections 32 and 33, township 129 north, range 78 west of the fifth principal meridian, Bates retraced west from this corner along the parallel to the Missouri River. He found that the timber, reported in the original field notes to be in sections 31 and 32, had been cleared off and that the bottom lands had grown up to dense rose brush, willows, and bullberry brush. None of the bearing trees cited in the original notes were standing, but he found enough evidence of the old corners to enable him to identify them. A meander corner had also been washed away. The

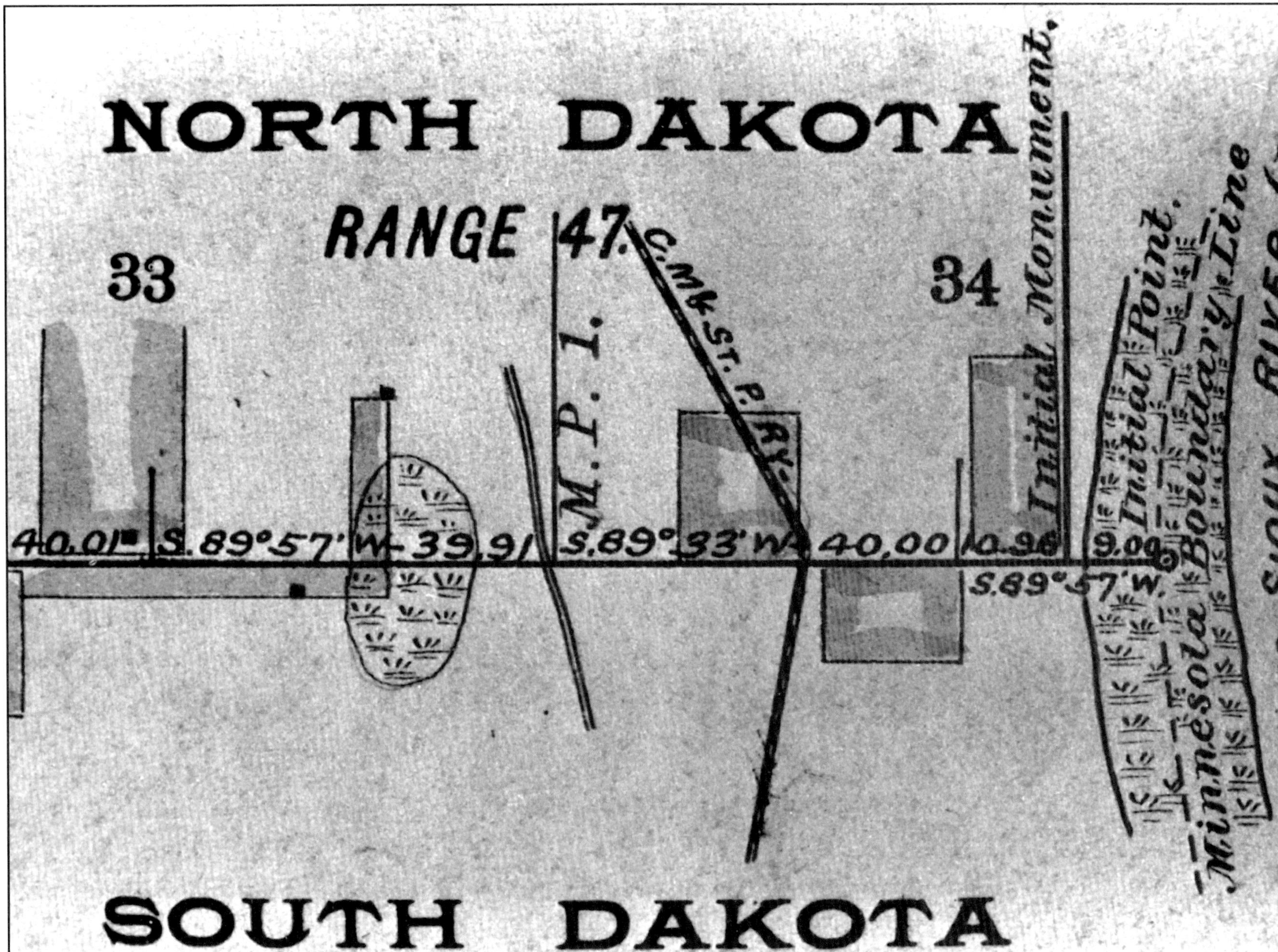

Bates' map showing the Bois des Sioux River and the location of the initial monument, drawn on the scale of two inches to a mile. South Dakota State Historical Society.

The initial monument, set 9 chains west of the juncture of the North Dakota, South Dakota, and Minnesota boundaries. Photo by the author.

river was frozen along its edges and running thick with anchor ice, so Bates did not attempt to get a line across or determine the distance to the west bank.

Returning to the corner for sections 32 and 33, Bates spent several days retracing east along the parallel, identifying and marking the old standard section and quarter section corners until he came to the corner for sections 31 and 32, township 129 north, range 54 west near the west boundary of the Sisseton and Wahpeton Indian Reservation. At this corner, on the evening of October 6, 1891, he observed the star Polaris for meridian, noted the time, and made his calculations to determine that the latitude was 45°55′ 15″ N. On the following morning, he turned off the azimuth 1°23′ to the west and, from the meridian so determined, turned off a right angle to the east and prolonged the line east on the tangent by double backsights and foresights across the Sisseton and Wahpeton Indian Reservation, making offsets from the tangent to the parallel.

As he proceeded east, Bates continued to take observations on Polaris on subsequent nights and to make offsets from the tangent to the parallel. In some instances, he found that the standard corners had been covered to the depth of a foot by a wagon road grade, but, when he located them, they were undisturbed and easily identified.

When Bates reached the Bois des Sioux River, he found it entirely dry and grown up to slough grass and reeds. Contrary to Commissioner Carter's expectations, there was no "main channel." In fact, wrote Bates, the river was "nothing but a marsh bed,

Main Street in White Rock, South Dakota, looking south, 1898. Randy M. Olson, Views of the Present . . . Visions of the Past.

which has been dry for several years." Bates could not find any traces of the meander corners on either the east or west sides of the river. He therefore went to the corner for sections 34 and 35, township 129 north, range 47 west in Minnesota and retraced the south boundary of section 34. At twelve chains, he intersected the east side of the Bois de Sioux River and at twenty-eight chains the west side of the river – or marsh bed – making the width of the river sixteen chains, or 1,056 feet.

Because the river was dry and possessed no well-defined channel or bed, Bates designated the center of the river as "the true point for the Initial Point, and point of commencement for the survey of the Boundary line between the States of North Dakota and South Dakota." Beginning at the initial point in the center of the river, Bates retraced the south boundary of section 34. Leaving the marshy river channel bearing north and south, he ascended gradually to the level prairie or bottom land.

At a point nine chains west of the initial point, on gently sloping ground about four feet above the river bed, and on what appeared to be permanent ground, Bates set three and one-half feet into the ground a quartzite monument seven feet long and ten inches square for "WITNESS INITIAL MONUMENT." The monument had been marked at the quarry according to the special instructions Bates had received from the General Land Office. The approximate latitude of the corner, according to Bates' survey notes, was 45°55' 15" N. From this corner, the railroad windmill in the town of White Rock, South Dakota, bore S.10°7' W.

White Rock was the point at which Bates received his mail and supplies while he was on the eastern end of the boundary. The 1892 *Travelers' Official Railway Guide* listed White Rock as being on the Fargo Line of the Chicago, Milwaukee & St. Paul Railway. On this road monuments were shipped from Sioux Falls to the boundary for placement on the eastern end of the state boundary.

White Rock was established in 1884 and was named after a huge granite boulder measuring five feet by eighteen feet that lay to the west of the proposed townsite. By 1887 the town boasted a population of fifty, a school, grain elevators, general merchandise stores, hotels, and a post office.

Just north of White Rock, the Bois des Sioux River forked and ran in two channels, one on either side of the town, until the channels came together south of town. The river channel was supposed to be the boundary between South Dakota and Minnesota, but the waters of the Bois des Sioux were fickle. At times, the volume of water and the strength of the current in the west channel indicated that it was the main channel, thus placing White Rock in Traverse County, Minnesota. At other times, the east channel appeared to be the main channel,

Residents of White Rock, South Dakota, posing on the large boulder after which the town was named. Randy M. Olson, Views of the Present . . . Visions of the Past.

The Bois des Sioux River as it appears today. Minnesota on the left, North and South Dakota on the right. Photo by the author.

Mile monument 4, the first one west of the initial monument that is still standing. Photo by the author.

thus placing White Rock in Roberts County, South Dakota. For some years, maps of Minnesota and South Dakota both located White Rock within their boundaries. When the location of the town once again became an issue in 1904, a court decision settled the dispute by a ruling that placed White Rock permanently in South Dakota.

The Bois des Sioux River today bears scant resemblance to what it was like when Bates visited it in 1891. A flood control project in 1940 dredged and straightened the shallow, meandering Bois des Sioux for nearly twenty-five miles of its length. And, alas, the rock for which White Rock was named also no longer exists. On May 20, 1899, it was blown "to smithereens" with a dynamite charge, according to the town's historian, and its rubble was used in the foundation for the Oscarson elevator.

At 19.96 chains west of the initial monument, Bates intersected the old standard quarter section corner and, although it had previously been considered unnecessary, here erected the first half-mile monument, marked at the quarry according to the instructions received from the General Land Office. At 15.52 chains west from the first half-mile monument, Bates crossed the Chicago, Milwaukee & St. Paul Railway, which turned to the northwest five chains north of this point. At forty chains west from the first half-mile monument, Bates came to the old standard corner to sections 33 and 34, township 129 north, range 47 west and here erected the first mile monument, marked 1 M on its east face, N.D. on its north face, and S.D. on its south face.

In accordance with his instructions and in keeping with surveying practices that had been established with the Land Ordinance of 1785 by which surveyors were required to note "the quality of the lands," Bates recorded the following in his field notes: "Land undulating prairie, subject to overflow. Soil, lst rate black loam." At long last, the project to mark the seventh standard parallel with "conspicuous monuments" was under way. As Bates and his crew moved west along the parallel, they left behind them at intervals of one-half mile hundreds of silent sentinels to guard Dakota's quartzite boundary.

At 61.33 chains west of the eleventh mile monument, Bates intersected the north boundary of the Sisseton and Wahpeton Indian Reservation. At 79.85 chains west of the eleventh mile monument, just short of the 80 chains that would have marked the distance as being a full mile, Bates set the twelfth mile monument. Because the monument marked an original survey – Bates was inside the Indian reservation – additional markings were required. The east face of the monument carried two grooves and the west face four grooves, to indicate the distance in miles to the last and to the next standard township corners.

Mile monuments 16 and 17 bear some of the few errors to be found on the monuments marking the boundary. Because monument 16 was set on a township corner and because it was within the Sisseton and Wahpeton Indian Reservation and thus on an original survey, it was to carry the range number on its east face (49) and on its west face (50). The township number (129) was to be placed on its north face.

The township number was not placed on the monument. Six grooves designating the distance to the last and next township corners were unnecessarily placed on both the east and west faces of the monument. The range numbers indicated that the monument was a township corner and the grooves were, therefore, not needed. Monument 17 bears on its north face the township number (129) that should have been placed on monument 16. Bates noted that monument 17 was placed in a "marshy bottom," where the soil would have been unstable. The monument is no longer standing. Perhaps livestock have trampled it down.

On October 30, 1891, the Lidgerwood *Broadaxe* noted that Bates and his crew had been camped in Lidgerwood the first part of the week and that they had subsequently moved to Rutland. Three weeks earlier, according to the LaMoure County *Chronicle,* the area had been visited by torrential rains that had filled sloughs, hampered travel, and halted fall plowing for the year.

Bates' work was being slowed for another reason as well. On October 13 Bates advised the General Land Office that he could not predict how much of the surveying and marking he could complete during the 1891 season because the monuments were not arriving on schedule at the shipping points and because "winter is liable to shut in at any time. . . . " It was about this same date that Bates recorded in

Mile monument 22, the first correctly marked township corner monument on the boundary, set where ranges 50 and 51 join. Photo by the author.

his notes that he was leaving the undulating prairie and ascending the Coteau des Prairie, a hilly and broken country cut with deep ravines containing oak, ash, and elm timber.

The Coteau des Prairie, or Prairie Hills, is that magnificent topographical feature with an elevation of over two thousand feet above sea level that extends from the North Dakota border southward as far as Lincoln County in southeastern South Dakota. On the northeastern edge of this rough highland, which possesses great religious significance for the Indians, a six hundred foot escarpment rises sharply above the Minnesota Valley and drops with equal abruptness into the James Basin on the west from an elevation of three hundred feet.

The rough, hilly area of the Coteau des Prairie is dotted with many lakes, some of which are deep and hold water even during the longest dry spells. Others are so shallow they hold water only during wet seasons. The town of Sisseton, in what was once the Sisseton and Wahpeton Indian Reservation, is nestled on the eastern edge of the Prairie Hills, which in this area are often shrouded with a bluish haze that seems to disappear as one approaches them. Bates set the monument marking the forty-third mile corner on top of a hill in the Coteau des Prairie, on the east edge of a deep ravine containing stands of oak, ash, and elm.

Bates recorded in his field notes that the land on the forty-fourth mile of the boundary was high and hilly with stony ridges. Monument 44 today is almost hidden by the rocks that someone has piled around it. Five chains west of this monument, Bates reached the top of the divide and began descending the west slope of the Coteau des Prairie. At 46.83 chains, he intersected the west boundary line of the Sisseton and Wahpeton Indian Reservation, and at 79.85 chains he set the monument marking the forty-fifth mile corner. Markings on this monument are in error. Being off the reservation, the monument is not on an original survey. The grooves placed on it indicating the distances to the preceding and subsequent township corners were, therefore, unnecessary. This monument, removed during a road construction project, is lying in a farmer's field.

In his field notes recording the information for the fifty-first mile, Bates wrote that from the half-mile monument he could see the grain elevator in Havana, North Dakota, on which he took a bearing. The land was once again gently rolling prairie and the soil "1st rate sandy loam." In the sixtieth mile, the boundary intersected the Chicago, Milwaukee & St. Paul Railway just north of the town of Newark, another of the points to which monuments could be shipped and from which they could be hauled by teams and wagons for distribution along the parallel. Here the country, no longer a part of the Indian reservation, was settled, and Bates recorded in his field notes the bearings from the monuments he set to fields, fences, barns, houses, and schools.

Bates set a total of 720 monuments along the boundary, and, of this number, only two could not be placed precisely at standard corners. One of these was the monument marking mile 78. The true point for the standard corner to sections 34 and 35, township 129 north, range 60 west was in the James River, where it could not be established.

Bates and his men waded the river, which at this point ran four feet deep between banks twelve feet high, and set the monument marking mile 78 on permanent ground "for witness to the 78th Mile Corner." Bates noted that the land at this point was "nearly level." Indeed it is. The James Valley is a broad, nearly level stretch of land from 50 to 75 miles wide and 250 miles long, so level, wrote E. P. Rothrock in *A Geology of South Dakota,* that "it takes water three weeks to travel the length of the state in the James River."

In range 66 west, Bates began "ascending over hilly country . . . " and his crew set the monument for mile 114 "on the top of the east slope of the Coteau du Missouri." The Coteau du Missouri, or Missouri Hills, is a belt of hill country east of the Missouri River that may be considered the transitional area in which the Prairie Plains merge into the Great Plains. The eastern border of the Missouri Hills is marked by moraines, or belts of glacial hills, and a fringe of high hills, separated by canyonlike valleys, forms the western edge of the Missouri Hills. Bates described the land as being "hilly and stony," containing some "fine springs of water."

This portion of the state boundary forms part of the base for the "German-Russian triangle," which extends from Dickey County to Hettinger County along the border. The triangle's apex is in Pierce and McHenry counties near the northern boundary of North Dakota. Included in the base is McIntosh County, which contains the highest concentration of German-Russians of any county in North Dakota.

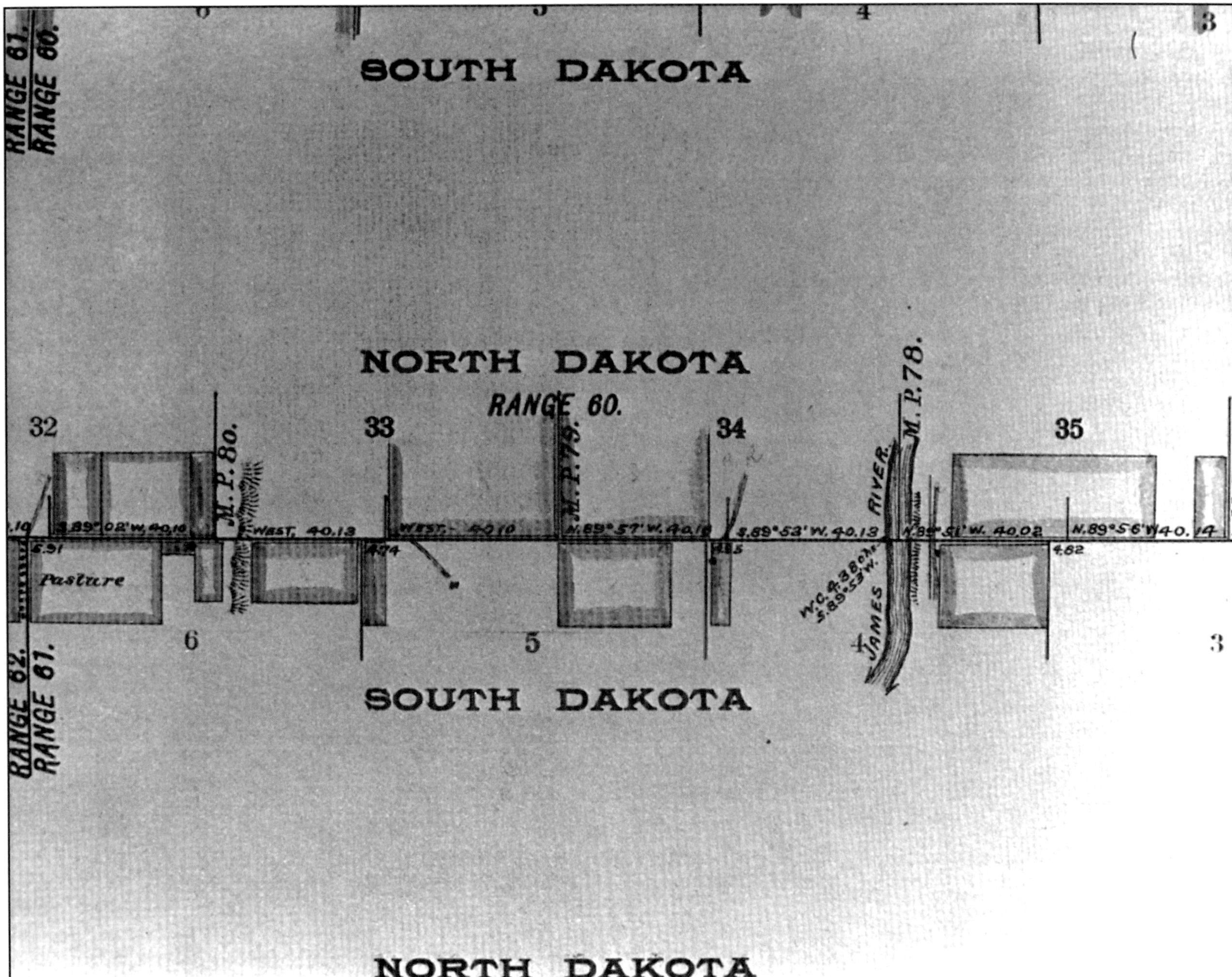

Bates' map of the boundary at its crossing of the James River. Included were sketches of pastures and cultivated fields, indicating that the country was settled. South Dakota State Historical Society.

Mile monument 169, broken off when hit by a running horse. Photo by the author.

Opened for settlement in 1884, McIntosh County contained 2,053 German-Russian settlers by 1890, the year before Bates passed through the area. Coming from south Russia to the Dakotas as late as they did, the German-Russians were forced to settle on the poorer, drier soils of the Coteau du Missouri and the Missouri Plateau.

As reported by the Winona *Times,* it was during the week of October 5-10, 1891, while Bates was in the area, that two of the last buffalo to be seen alive and in the wild in McIntosh County were sighted. Men gave chase and got close enough to the animals to strike them with their whips and pitchforks, but no one had a gun with which to kill them. The same newspaper in its issue of August 18, 1892, reported that the two buffalo had eventually been captured.

The last point along the boundary to which Bates could ship monuments on the Chicago, Milwaukee & St. Paul Railway was Eureka, a center of German-Russian settlement about a dozen miles south of the boundary and about four times that distance east of the Missouri River. The monuments and the survey were newsworthy, so as the three carloads of monuments destined for Eureka made their way along the Roscoe Line of the James River Division, such newspapers as the Frederick *Free Press* reported their progress and such papers as the Pierre *Daily Capital* and the Bismarck *Daily Tribune* reprinted the stories.

The three carloads of stone monuments arrived in Roscoe, South Dakota, from the east on Tuesday, November 10, and were sidetracked at the station until they could be shipped north. The three railroad cars would have contained about eighty-five to ninety monuments, enough for the forty-five miles of the boundary between Eureka and the Missouri River. From the size and weight of the monuments, exclaimed the Roscoe *Herald,* "it may be presumed that when once in place they will remain undisturbed until the time when we are called out of our graves to attend the proceedings of the Day of Judgement." Once the three cars of what the Eureka *Independent* described as "Sioux Falls granite" had arrived in Eureka, Ben Haggard got the contract to haul the monuments to the state line.

Included in this shipment would have been the monument to mark mile 169. Bates recorded in his field notes that a wagon road running along the line at this point turned into one running north and south. Today, monument 169 is broken off slightly below ground level and lies just east of Highway 83. According to local lore, a horse struck the monument while on a dead run on a dark winter night and broke it off. The horse died as a result of the accident.

The monument to mark mile 170 would also have been included in those shipped to Eureka. Originally, this monument had little besides its mile number to distinguish it from any other. It was set, noted Bates, on "gently rolling prairie." Today, however, the monument bears an inscription in addition to the one placed on it at the Sioux Falls quarry. The monument bears on its east face the initials "J 0 E S" and the date "1930." Each Sunday in the summer of 1930, a young fellow and his girl drove to this monument in a Model T Ford. During the summer, the fellow carved the inscription on the monument.

After Bates had finished his retracing of the seventh standard parallel east from the Missouri River and had set the initial monument, he did not record any dates in his

Mile monument 170, on which a young man added his own markings in 1930. Photo by the author.

field notes until he stopped work for the season on November 21. One cannot determine, therefore, how many miles he covered nor how many monuments he set on a given day. The men must have worked quickly and efficiently, however. They covered the 190 miles between the Bois des Sioux and Missouri rivers and erected slightly more than 380 monuments in about six weeks. On October 6 Bates had observed the star Polaris for meridian and in mid-October the crew had camped near Lidgerwood.

Bates reported to the Yankton *Press and Dakotan* when he had finished work for the season that the surface of the country through which the seventh standard parallel ran east of the Missouri River was "almost dead level. . . . " He made good time. On November 6 Bates informed the General Land Office (his post office address was now Eureka, McPherson County, South Dakota) that he expected to reach the Missouri River "with the 'state line' complete" about November 18 or 20.

The steamboat Rosebud *"homeward bound" on the Upper Missouri River. Elwyn B. Robinson Department of Special Collections, Chester Fritz Library, University of North Dakota.*

The Winona *Times* on November 12 described the beautiful weather that had allowed farmers to complete their fall work – the temperature had reached 80°F on October 29 according to the *Records from Fort Yates*. But the surveying season was well advanced. According to the *Records from Fort Yates,* the steamer *Rosebud* had arrived on the morning of November 9 and had left for Bismarck that evening. She was the last boat for the season. The LaMoure County *Chronicle* on November 27, 1891, reported that the steamboat *Abner Neal* was icebound about twenty miles north of Bismarck with a cargo of wheat.

On the night of November 11-12, an unexpected blizzard with heavy snow and driving winds struck the area along both sides of the state boundary for some distance both east and west of the Missouri River. Threshing was stopped for the season and farmers lost many head of livestock. Roads were badly drifted and almost impassable. The Napoleon *Homestead* began its account of the storm with the understatement that "We've been having winter in earnest the past 10 days." The mail team from Steele had been unable to get through, and the Ashley mail was late. The winds were so strong and the snow so heavy that no one dared to be on the roads. The LaMoure County *Chronicle* reported trains stopped on the rails by high drifts. Plows sent from Jamestown to clear the tracks had also become stuck in the snow. The Frederick *Free Press* described the blizzard as "an old fashioned snow storm," unusual in its severity for being the first storm of the season. (It was not all bad, however. The deep snow provided better sleighing than there had been for years.)

North Dakota Geological Survey camp, showing tent and equipment similar to what Bates and his survey crew would have used. Elwyn B. Robinson Department of Special Collections, Chester Fritz Library, University of North Dakota.

On November 13, John Dolan, "a destitute citizen," was admitted to the post hospital at Fort Yates suffering from severe frostbite of hands and feet. Doctors had to amputate four fingers on his right hand and three on his left. Dolan also lost his left foot above the ankle and all the toes on his right foot. Snow drifts around Winona and Fort Yates were five to fifteen feet deep. Heavy ice was forming on the Missouri River, and by November 19 the river was completely frozen over with ice six inches thick. A few days previous to this, John Waldon of Winona had lost a fine cow through an air hole in the ice.

In his more than twenty years of surveying the public domain in Dakota, Bates had learned that he could usually count on having working weather until about Christmas. The blizzard of November 11-12 in 1891, however, caught him and his men in western McPherson County with fifty miles of the boundary yet to mark and about one hundred monuments yet to set. On November 27 the Yankton *Press and Dakotan* carried an account of the men's experiences during the storm.

One of the crew's two tents was blown down during the first night of the blizzard, and the men huddled together in the one remaining. They tied themselves together with a piece of rope two hundred feet long and all night long hugged the ground, expecting at any moment that the wind would carry the tent away. Their intention was to remain together until the rope broke, but, fortunately, they were spared that test. When dawn came and they could see, the men made their way to the sod house of a German-Russian settler, where they remained until the storm had blown itself out. They rounded up their livestock and gathered up their equipment. Over the last fifty miles of the boundary the men worked in snow, which in places had been blown into drifts eight to ten feet deep. On the bottom land of the Missouri River, the snow was from two to four feet deep.

The terrain was also becoming more difficult to negotiate. Bates was recording "gravelly ridges and benches" and "stony ridges" and "some oak brush in ravines" in his field notes. After setting the monument to mark mile 185, he noted that he was leaving "high broken stony hills" and "descending to the Missouri river bottoms." From mile monument 188, Bates made his way through bottom land grown up to willow, bullberry, box elder, and rose brush. From this point to the bank of the river, the land was a sandy bottom subject to overflow; the soil was sandy and second to third rate.

The monument to mark mile 190 was the last one Bates' crew set east of the river. From this monument, Bates measured west 3.80 chains to the river bank, twenty feet high at this point, and 8.25 chains to the edge of the water in the main channel of the river. "Owing to the lateness of the season, Nov. 18th," Bates wrote in his field notes, "and the extreme cold weather and deep snow, work for the season was discontinued at the 190th Mile monument."

In his field notes, which he eventually sent to the General Land Office in Washington, Bates explained why he had pursued the work of surveying and marking the seventh standard parallel as he had during the 1891 season. Fearing that snow would obscure the old standard corners, he had begun at the east bank of the Missouri River rather than near the Sisseton and Wahpeton Indian Reservation as instructed and had "pressed the retracements first, marking the old cors., so they could be found if covered with snow." The monuments were set after the retracements had been made. It was well that he had taken this precaution, Bates wrote, because the "violent snow storm" of November would otherwise have stopped work for the season. It would have been impossible to execute retracements through snow drifts eight to ten feet deep.

Bates also included in his field notes a description of the country through which his crew had passed while executing the retracements and setting the monuments. For the most part, the land had been covered with a good growth of wild grasses. From the Sisseton and Wahpeton Indian Reservation to the Coteau du Missouri, the country was thickly settled, and the crops in 1891 proved that the soil would support farming. Bates had passed through "thrifty settlements of Hollanders and Russians" who were making a success of farming and who had raised twenty to forty bushels of wheat to the acre in 1891.

Bates had found surface water to be very scarce along the entire boundary. One drain in the Sisseton and Wahpeton Indian Reservation in the thirty-seventh mile contained water in holes. On the west slope of the Coteau des Prairie, some ravines contained springs. Only in the James River was there water in any appreciable amount. Maple Creek, the drain in the ninety-seventh mile, and Elm Creek had contained water in holes. Bates had found several springs in the ravines between miles 113 and 114 and a few waterholes in creeks between miles 180 and 181. The crew located no more water until mile 186, where it stood in pools in a creek bed. There were a great many water courses and lake beds along the boundary that gave the appearance of having once contained water, but they had all been dry. Bates credited the scarcity of surface water to the "continuous drought" that had prevailed for the past several years.

On November 19 Bates took the final oath of his assistants, all of whom had remained with him from September 19, when they had begun the retracements, until he discharged them. Bates gave November 21 as the date on which he stopped work for the season. He then hurried south to warmer weather and arrived in Yankton on the night of November 25. Bates had completed the permanent survey and marking of the boundary from Minnesota to the Missouri River and now, declared the Yankton *Press and Dakotan*, "the record is complete and enduring and will defy the ravages of time until the heavens roll up as a scroll and the earth returns to its nebulous state. After these events half mile posts on the plains of the Dakotas will be of no special utility to the wayfarer."

Chapter 6

From Monument 190 to the Terminal Monument

"Superb scratching posts for cattle. . . . "
Charles H. Bates

During the surveying season of 1892, a leap year, and the four hundredth anniversary of Columbus' discovery of America, Charles H. Bates surveyed and marked the seventh standard parallel between the Missouri River and the Montana border. He spent the preceding winter in Yankton and devoted a part of his time to writing up his field notes from the previous season. Bates informed Commissioner Carter at the General Land Office by letter on March 23, 1892, that he was sending by the Adams Express Company a box containing triplicate copies of the field notes of the survey and retracement of the boundary between North and South Dakota from the initial point to mile 190 and also triplicate sets of plats of the boundary.

Bates also spent much time preparing for the 1892 surveying season, fretting about the delays caused by the weather, and importuning the General Land Office to send him the special instructions without which he could not complete the surveying and marking of the Dakota boundary west of the Missouri River. He also requested, several times – each time with no results – that the General Land Office pay him for the surveying he had completed during the 1891 season.

Upon completion of the surveying and marking of the boundary east of the Missouri River, Bates was eligible to receive a payment of ninety percent of the stipulated compensation, once the work had been examined and approved. When the compensation was not forthcoming, Bates became increasingly impatient. Considering the amount of money he had invested and the rate of interest he was paying on what he had borrowed, the delay in being paid was working a hardship on him.

In a letter dated January 7, 1892, Carter reminded Bates that he could not be paid until his work had been examined and accepted. The examination had not been ordered because "earnest efforts to secure the services of a competent person to perform the duty" had thus far been unsuccessful. Bates was assured that everything possible was being done to have his work examined and that he would be paid once that was done.

Assurances do not, however, pay bills. It was not until October 25, 1892, that D. A. Ray, principal clerk of surveys, submitted the papers authorizing that Bates receive ninety percent on account for the work he had done in 1891. Ray requested "early attention to the case, as this matter has been unavoidably delayed several months."

Nothing frustrated Bates more than the delay in receiving from the General Land Office the special instructions regarding the surveying and marking of the seventh standard parallel from mile 190 to the Montana border. He could not arrange transportation for the monuments until they had been marked at the quarry. And the monuments could not be marked until he had received the special instructions.

To keep the General Land Office informed as to his whereabouts, Bates had written to Carter shortly after he had returned to Yankton in November 1891. In the same letter, he asked that instructions for the line west of the Missouri River be sent to him "at an *early* date," because he wanted to begin work as early as possible in the spring. On January 6, 1892, Bates wrote to Carter again, complaining that he had not received his special instructions.

On January 7 Carter informed Bates that the supplemental instructions could not be prepared until his office knew, "with as much accuracy" as possible, the latitude of the point at which the seventh standard parallel crossed the Missouri River. When this information was received, the instructions would be "promptly prepared and sent." Bates immediately supplied the requested information. "As near as I could interpolate it," he wrote to Carter on January 13, 1892, the latitude of the point was 45° 55′ 20″ N.

When Bates wrote Carter on January 18, again requesting his instructions, he was informed that the special instructions would be mailed during the week of January 26. The delay in receiving his special instructions caused Bates anxiety because he feared that he might not be able to complete the survey within the time period specified in his contract and he would therefore be liable to forfeiture of his bond. He wrote to Carter on March 2 and again on March 23, stressing the necessity of receiving the instructions "as *soon* as possible" so that he might complete all necessary arrangements and get into the field as soon as weather permitted.

The special instructions, which Bates finally received under the date of March 23, were in three parts. The first part specified that Bates, at the crossing of the Missouri River, had to use at least "two independent well-conditioned triangles" to determine the distance across the river. He was to insert the computations and illustrative diagrams in his field notes.

The second part of the special instructions dealt with the survey of the seventh standard parallel, which west of the

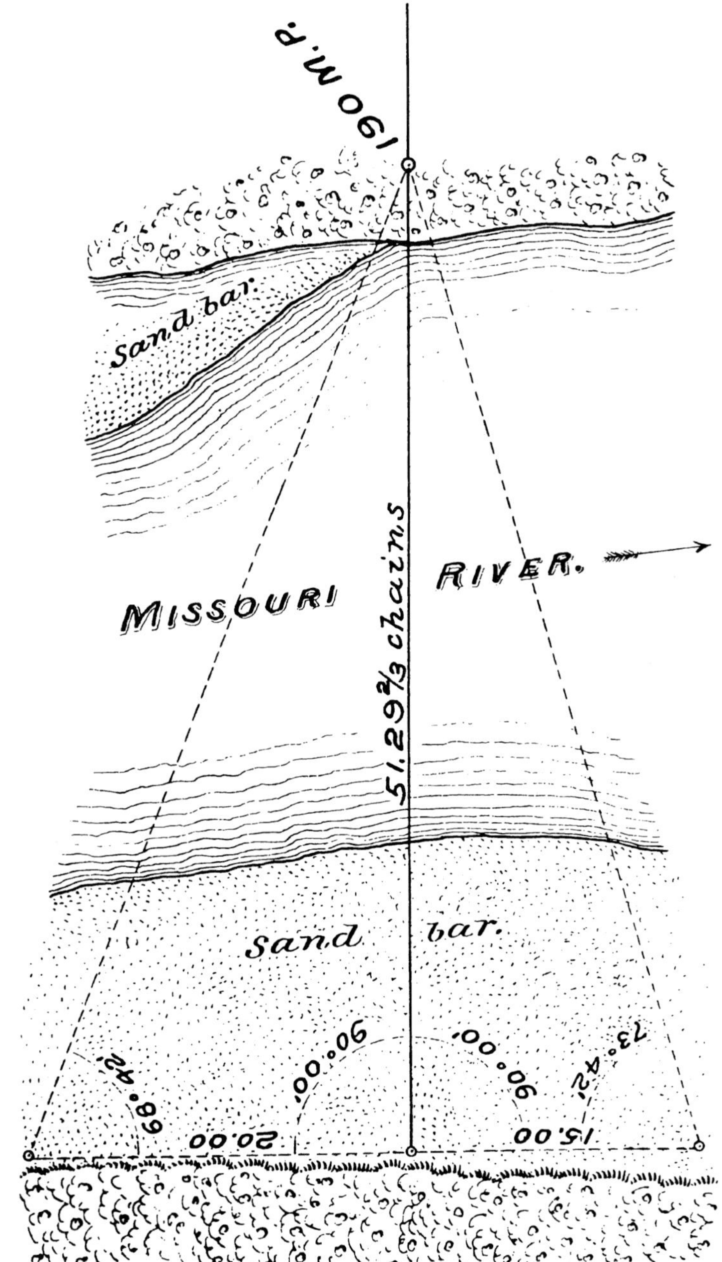

Diagram illustrating the method by which Bates determined the width of the Missouri River. South Dakota State Historical Society.

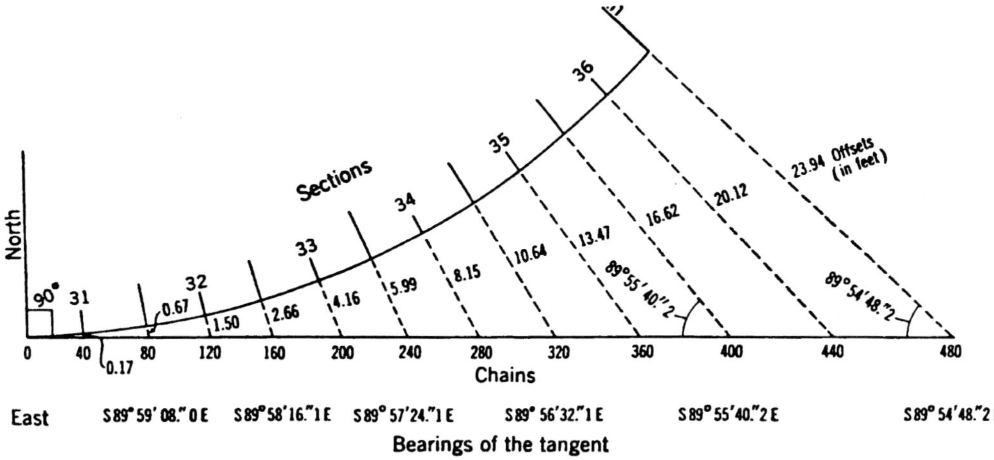

Illustration depicting tangent method of establishing a parallel of latitude. Philip Kissam, Surveying for Civil Engineers, *© 1956, p. 319. Reproduced with permission by McGraw-Hill Book Company, Inc.*

Missouri River was not to be a retracement of a survey already completed, but an original survey. The great length of this section of the boundary, about 170 miles from the river to the Montana border, required a survey by offsets from the tangent to the parallel, using a first-class transit and prolongation of the line by double backsights and foresights.

The survey of standard parallels by offsets from tangents was theoretically correct and lent itself well to surveys of short distances over open and level, or gently rolling, ground. This method had drawbacks, however, especially when used in rough terrain and through dense brush. This method was also time consuming, and any error, even a slight one, was perpetuated, resulting in a significant distortion of the survey at its completion.

A clerk at the General Land Office had developed an improved survey method – actually a modification of the tangent method – using a secant line through any two standard corners on the parallel, four miles apart, thereby reducing the greatest actual offset to less than one seventh of that required in connection with a tangent. The new method and its application to the survey of the seventh standard parallel west of the Missouri River were explained to Bates, and Carter recommended that he use it.

Among the advantages of the secant method for determining a parallel of latitude were that it could be used in all kinds of terrain; it was faster and eliminated work, such as clearing brush; it was less subject to error; and it permitted surveying to be done when the sun was obscured by clouds, haze, or smoke because directions did not have to be fixed by solar apparatus alone. Tables I and II of the *Manual of Surveying Instruction* were to be used in conjunction with the new method in order to determine true directions, on condition that observations on Polaris at elongation be made once in each stretch of thirty-six miles.

After studying the materials that Carter had sent to him, Bates was of the opinion that the method of laying off the parallel from a secant line would prove far superior to the old method of offsetting from a tangent line. He proposed to run the original survey from the Missouri River to the Montana border using the secant method.

Bates was also instructed to indicate on his maps all topographical features for a half mile on each side of the boundary. In his field notes, he had to give true bearings, when such data could be secured without causing delay in the survey, to such prominent distant objects as conspicuous

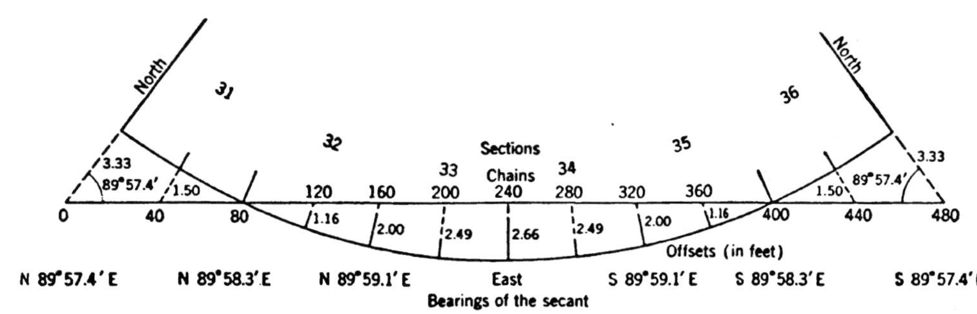

Illustration depicting secant method of establishing a parallel of latitude. Philip Kissam, Surveying for Civil Engineers, *© 1956, p. 325. Reproduced with permission by McGraw-Hill Book Company, Inc.*

buttes and groves of trees (suggesting the presence of water). At the point at which the parallel crossed the meridians of 102° and 103° west longitude from Greenwich, Bates was to establish corners (marked by stone if practicable), similar to closing township corners as per requirements contained in the *Manual of Surveying Instructions.* Specific instructions were included for marking the stones.

Part three of Bates' instructions covered the monuments that were to be set on the newly surveyed parallel. The mile and one-half mile monuments were the same as those used east of the river, and the markings would be the same as those used for monuments on the Sisseton and Wahpeton Indian Reservation.

The terminal monument, the same size as the others, was to be established at the intersection of the seventh standard parallel with the east boundary of Montana and set with its faces directed to the cardinal points. The east face of the monument was to bear the date 1892, the initials "T. M." for Terminal Monument, and the total distance between the initial and terminal monuments, known to be slightly more than 360 miles. A vertical groove on both the north and south faces of the monument and marked with the letters "By." would indicate the boundary of the Dakotas with Montana. The north and south faces would also carry the initials "N.D." and "S.D.," respectively, for the states. The abbreviation "Mont." was to be placed on the west face of the monument. Bates improved on these instructions and added his name to the west face, as well as his title of United States surveyor.

Commissioner Carter concluded the special instructions by expressing the hope that Bates would "survey the 7th Standard Parallel with an accuracy sufficient to make it available as a base from which to correct the maps of North and South Dakota."

Having received the special instructions, Bates could now complete the arrangements for marking and shipping the monuments. In late April, according to the Yankton *Press and Dakotan,* Bates had travelled to Sioux Falls for this purpose.

According to newspaper accounts and the records of the Benton Transportation Company, the monuments used to mark the seventh standard parallel west of the Missouri River were shipped by rail from Sioux Falls to Pierre, South Dakota, and thence to the boundary by steamboat. Five rail cars of monuments, a total of 170 monuments, were shipped on the steamer *Rosebud* to St. Benedict, an Indian mission located in Kenel, a town located some eighteen miles by river below Fort Yates. Kenel was on the west bank of the Missouri River a short distance from the boundary. Six cars of monuments, a total of 176 monuments, were shipped to Dickinson, North Dakota, via the Missouri River and the Northern Pacific Railroad.

From 1885 to the 1930s, according to William E. Lass in his *History of Steamboating on the Upper Missouri River,* Isaac P. Baker had almost complete control of the commercial shipping on the Upper Missouri. In 1885 the Fort Benton Transportation Company, which had been founded by T. C. Power in 1875, was reorganized as the Benton Transportation Company. Actual management of the company was in the hands of Baker who was the general agent and one-sixth owner of the firm. Declining business on the river above Fort Buford, which had been built three miles below the mouth of the Yellowstone River in 1866, led Baker to concentrate his boats in a smaller trade area. In the spring of 1892, Baker informed Captain Charles W. Powell, United States army engineer, that in the future his boats would ply the Upper Missouri between Pierre and the Fort Berthold Indian Agency. After this date, Baker seldom sent a boat to any point above Fort Buford.

Baker continued to participate in the downriver trade between Bismarck and Pierre through the navigation season of 1895. Boats from Bismarck usually carried general merchandise and coal for the various settlements, army posts, and Indian agencies. Boats picked up cargoes of grain, hides, buffalo bones, potatoes, and wool, which were consigned to the railhead at Pierre. At Pierre the Benton Transportation Company boats would again be loaded with merchandise and coal for points as far downstream as Fort Randall. On the return trip, boats picked up freight for points between Pierre and Bismarck.

During the first half of the 1890s, the bulk of the steamboat commerce on the Upper Missouri was carried on the Bismarck-Pierre section of the river. In 1892 Baker operated only two steamers, the *Rosebud* and the *F. Y. Batchelor.* His attempt to sell one of the boats in 1894 suggests that the company's business had declined to the point where it could be handled by a single boat.

Shipping on the Missouri River was not without its hazards, because, as Stanley Vestal wrote in his book *The Missouri,* "The trouble with going up the Missouri River in a boat is that you have to take the boat along." The Bismarck *Settler* reported a case in point on August 25, 1892. A few days previously and a few miles north of Chamberlain, the *Rosebud* had hit a snag that tore a large hole in her bottom. She sank in shallow water, but was later raised, repaired, and returned to service.

Originating in the union of three sizable streams in southwestern Montana – the Jefferson, Madison, and Gallatin rivers – the Missouri River tumbles, slides, meanders, sidesteps, and plays leapfrog for almost 2,500 miles until it joins the Mississippi just above St. Louis. It is, wrote Vestal, "an honest-to-God American river – *the* American river. No other river was ever so dead-set against being navigated. No other river was ever so determined on having its own way." Father Marquette, who reached its mouth in June 1673, was the first white man to see the mouth of the Missouri and to leave a record of it. He wrote that he had never seen anything more frightful, and boatmen on the river shared his sentiments. Probably no other highway of its length on the continent has been the object of such violent and heartfelt cursing.

George Fitch wrote in his delightful article entitled "The Missouri River" that there is only one river like the Missouri – a river with personality, habits, dissipations, a sense of humor, and a woman's caprice. The Missouri travels sideways, interferes in politics, rearranges geography, and dabbles in real estate. The Missouri "plays hide and seek with you to-day and to-morrow follows you around like a pet dog with a dynamite cracker tied to its tail." About the Missouri, the Sioux City *Register* wrote in 1868, "Of all the variable things in creation the most uncertain are the action of a jury, the state of a woman's mind, and the condition of the Missouri River."

A river with the peculiarities and fickleness of the Missouri demanded special qualities of a steamboat that had the temerity to try navigating it. A Missouri River steamboat had to be shallow, lithe, deep-chested, and exceedingly strong in the stern wheel. It should be hinged in the middle so it could negotiate sharp bends in the river and fitted with a suction dredge so that when it could not climb over a sandbar it could assimilate it. The Missouri River steamboat should be able to make use of a channel, but it should not have to depend upon it. Fitch observed that a steamer that could not, on occasion, "climb a steep clay bank, go across a cornfield and corner a river that is trying to get away, has little excuse for trying to navigate the Missouri."

The Missouri River once teemed with steamboats. Business was good and profits were high. Of course, there was the occasional embarrassing occurrence. Sometimes a boat would have a long passenger list for a town and not be able to find it, the river

The Rosebud, *a Missouri River steamboat, on which monuments were shipped to the boundary between North and South Dakota. South Dakota State Historical Society.*

having either removed the town or run away from it over night. And sometimes the river would sneak away from a steamboat that had been tied up on its bank over night. Nevertheless, the steamboat business on the Missouri flourished until the coming of the railroads.

The *Rosebud* was among the steamboats with the qualities necessary to ply the Missouri River. She was 193 feet long, had a beam of 33 feet, and her hold was 3 feet 3 inches deep. Among the oldest boats on the river – she had been used as a transport by Generals Crook and Terry in the Indian war of 1876 – the *Rosebud* had the lightest draft of any boat of her tonnage on the Missouri. She had a carrying capacity of 286 tons. At 182 tons loaded, she drew three feet of water; at seventy-five tons loaded, she drew two feet. Empty, the *Rosebud* drew only seventeen inches of water, almost making a truism of the claim that a Missouri River steamboat could navigate on a heavy dew. During most of the navigation season on the river, steamboat men could not depend on the channel being any more than three feet deep.

The *Rosebud's* more than twenty years of service on the Missouri attest to her ability to accommodate the whims of this rogue river. But, in the end, the river bested her. In the spring of 1896 the *Rosebud* and the *F. Y. Batchelor* were moored at the Bismarck landing. A rise in the river floated the *Rosebud* over the piling and on May 21 a sudden fall in the river dropped her on the piles, stoving in her bottom timbers. A futile effort was made to pump the water out, but only the machinery could be saved. The once-proud *Rosebud* was dismantled so as not to obstruct navigation.

Another peculiarity of the Missouri River, before its personality was altered by dams, was that it had two annual rises, and Bates timed his shipment of the monuments to take advantage of them. The first rise, the April rise, occurred anytime from mid-March to mid-April and was the result of melting snow on the lower slopes of the Rocky Mountains and on the northern Great Plains and the early spring rains that occur from the Dakotas southward. By mid-May, the April rise had usually declined on the Upper Missouri.

The second rise, the June rise, occurred any time from mid-May to around July 1 and was caused by the melting of the high-altitude Rocky Mountain snows and the late spring rains on the plains. Sometimes, as in 1863, there was no rise. Sometimes, as in 1881, there were uncontrollable floods. Usually, however, the two rises were moderate, providing an almost continuous navigation season from mid-March to late June. After the June rise, the river dropped sharply because of the lack of significant rainfall during the late summer and fall in the country through which the river flowed.

The April rise of the Missouri River in 1892 was late because the cold spring delayed the melting of snow at the headwaters of all the river's tributary streams. The Pierre *Daily Capital* on April 26 observed that the river was extremely low. A month later, on May 27, the paper noted that the river still had not risen. At the same time the year before, the river had been six to seven feet above low water mark and had remained high, varying from six to ten feet above low water mark, up to July 1.

Despite the low water, the freighting season had begun. According to records from the adjutant general's office, the ice on the Missouri River at Fort Yates began running on March 29. The *Rosebud,* the first boat of the season, arrived at the fort on the evening of April 16. Under the command of Captain John Belks, the *Rosebud* returned to Pierre on the morning of April 29 and began taking on cargo. Included in the freight was a large amount of government goods bound for Fort Yates, as well as five carloads of monuments that had been lying on the wharf awaiting shipment to the state boundary.

According to the records of the Benton Transportation Company, the 170 boundary monuments taken on board the *Rosebud* at Pierre had a combined weight of 135,200 pounds, just under an average of 800 pounds apiece. The freight rate was 25 cents per 100 pounds, making a total freight cost of $338.00 for shipping the monuments to their destination at St. Benedict. The 170 monuments would be enough to cover 85 miles of the boundary, to a point about five miles east of present-day White Butte, South Dakota, which would be 275 miles west of the initial monument.

St. Benedict's Mission, established in 1878 and located in the town of Kenel, was slightly more than two miles south of the Dakota border and on the west bank of the river. Kenel was some eighteen miles by river below Fort Yates and was a sub-issue station for the Standing Rock Indian Reservation. Kenel was named for Father Martin Kenel, a Benedictine priest who came to the mission in 1884 and who served for many years as the superintendent of the boarding school and then of the industrial school when the institution was taken over by the United States government.

Shrine and church at Kenel, South Dakota. South Dakota State Historical Society.

Kenel was a small town with a trader's store, in which the post office was located, and a large Catholic church. The United States government eventually took over the boarding school and converted it into a government industrial school. Later, when Benedictine Sisters arrived, girls were admitted. Father Kenel retired in October 1906, and the government named the school the Martin Kenel Agricultural School in his honor. When the school was closed in 1919, some of the buildings were dismantled and moved to Fort Yates. Both the mission and the original town of Kenel now lie under the waters of the Oahe Reservoir.

According to the Pierre *Daily Capital,* the *Rosebud* left Pierre on the afternoon of May 1, a Sunday, bound for points upriver. Two days later, on May 3, the *Rosebud* had arrived at Forest City, a town midway between Pierre and Mobridge, lying on the left bank of the river, across from the Cheyenne Agency. The Forest City *Capital* reported that the *Rosebud* had a large cargo on board, including seed grain for the agency, some brick and lumber for the construction of the Catholic church at Forest City, and a large number of stone monuments to be set on the boundary between North and South Dakota. The *Rosebud* completed her trip to Fort Yates, returned to Pierre on May 9, and left with another cargo on May 10.

In early June, according to the Pierre *Daily Capital,* the Missouri River at Pierre had begun its June rise. At noon on June 3, the river registered 4.3 feet above low water mark, having risen 3 feet during the previous 48 hours. At noon on June 4, the river registered 5.1 feet above low water mark, a rise of nearly a foot in twenty-four hours. By June 10, the river level had reached a point 9 feet above the low water mark, higher than it had been since 1883, and it was still rising.

The Pierre *Daily Capital* on June 7 described the river as being on a rampage. Shippers were fearful that their boats would get hung up on sandbars. High water washed out the approach on the south end of the pontoon bridge at Pierre, and the river cut a channel through the island that lay opposite the city. The *Jim Leighton* landed near the foot of Pierre Street on June 8 and would have to continue making landings there as long as the high water continued.

The high water was an aid to shipping, however, and the manifests of the Benton Transportation Company reveal that the freight business was good. Included in the freight handled was that consigned to Bates. The *Rosebud* picked up supplies in Bismarck to be shipped to him at St. Benedict. Albright and West consigned 69 packages of groceries, a total of 4,735 pounds. Freight cost was 40 cents per 100 pounds, for a total of $18.94. Also included in the shipment for Bates were 178 sacks of oats, a total of 15,985 pounds, on which the freight was $63.94. The Bismarck Grain and Produce Company also shipped oats to Bates, 32 sacks, on which the freight bill was $11.20.

After leaving Bismarck and stopping at St. Benedict, the *Rosebud* arrived in Pierre on the night of June 10 and began taking on freight the next morning. Included in the cargo, according to the Pierre *Daily Capital* for June 11, were the monuments destined for the state boundary that Bates had consigned. The *Rosebud* was scheduled to leave for upriver from Pierre on June 12.

The *Rosebud's* departure was delayed, first to June 13, and then to the night of June 14, because the engineer had been called to Cincinnati by the serious illness of his wife. A replacement licensed engineer did not arrive until June 14. A few days later, according to the Mound City *Journal* on June 17, the monuments reached LaGrace, South Dakota, on their way to Dickinson. LaGrace was located near the mouth of Spring Creek and had been platted in 1883. The town had a newspaper, a post office, and a telegraph station. LaGrace was the first county seat of Campbell County, and for many years it was one of the busiest steamboat stops between Bismarck and Chamberlain.

The Dickinson *Press* on June 18, 1892, reported that six cars of monuments, 176 monuments, had arrived in the city, consigned to A. C. McGillivray. "Senator" McGillivray, as he was known, was a staunch Republican and owner of a large general merchandise business who frequently advertised his wares in the Dickinson *Press*. McGillivray also owned a large ranch near Dickinson and had one of the fastest trotting horses in the state. The animal was entered in races as far east as Fargo.

In May 1891 an injunction had been served against McGillivray as owner and manager of the Dickinson Coal Mining Company. According to the Lidgerwood *Broadaxe* for May 22, 1891, the owner of the land on which the mine was located had complained of not being paid his stipulated royalty. With the injunction, work at the mine ceased. The company had just received a big contract from the Jamestown Electric Company for coal and was therefore a good deal embarrassed.

On June 25 McGillivray placed an advertisement in the Dickinson *Press*–"Someone who wants a big hauling contract should see A. C. McGillivray"–inviting bids for hauling 176 stone monuments to the state line near the Cave Hills in northwestern South Dakota. J. H. Colgrove was the successful bidder, and for three weeks beginning on July 23 he ran the following advertisement in the Dickinson *Press:* "Wanted–three or four teams to haul granite posts to the state line, by the day or by the piece." Three monuments weighed about 2,400 pounds, and over the rough country between Dickinson and the state line would be a good load for two horses. Five monuments weighed about 4,000 pounds and made a good load for four horses.

Colgrove was an enterprising man–he had an electric bell installed for communication between his house and barn–who was involved in a number of businesses in Dickinson. He had a blacksmith shop and advertised a full line of materials with which to repair wagons. He also sold wagons, buggies, and farm machinery. He owned a ranch and a livery stable and had the contract for burying dead animals found in the town and surrounding area. In September 1892 he became the agent for the East Lehigh coal mine and advertised coal for $2.00 per ton, delivered.

Had the hopes and expectations of the New England Colony Association for Dakota materialized, the monuments could have been transported by rail from Dickinson to the boundary rather than by Colgrove's horses and wagons. The Colony Association, which had been organized in Boston, obtained an option on all railroad lands in Hettinger County and on the two tiers of townships adjoining Hettinger County on the west. New England City was established in 1887. The townsite was some twenty-five miles south of Dickinson and on the north bank of the Cannonball River. A post office was established in 1887; and mail was brought down from Dickinson two to three times per week and distributed to stations at Grand River, Cave Hills, and Ashcroft on the Little Missouri.

Two railroads were expected to reach New England City in the spring of 1888. One railroad was surveyed through the county from Mandan to the Black Hills, and another was projected from Dickinson south through the site for New England City to a junction with the Black Hills line. Neither had been built by 1892, when they would have made so much easier the transport of the boundary monuments.

New England City was once a lively place, especially during the Messiah Craze of 1890 when it served as a military supply depot and headquarters for troops that were sent to the town during the Indian scare. The town boasted a newspaper–the *Rainy Buttes Sentinel*–several stores, and rooming houses. But, apart from a few large, widely spaced ranches, the area around New England City was virtually uninhabited, and after the scare the town declined until it sustained a revival during the Second Dakota Boom. When Bates and his crew were in the area, only a single store, the post office, and a rooming house remained open. More than anything else, the abandonment of plans to build a railroad from Dickinson through New

England City to the Black Hills accounts for the Colony Association's hopes and expectations being dashed.

Whether moved by railroad, steamboat, or horse-drawn wagons, the monuments had it easier getting to their destination on the boundary in 1892 than Bates did. Cold, wet, windy weather repeatedly delayed his departure from Yankton. The years before and including 1890 were drought years. The Missouri River at Pierre was so low and the sandbars so close together that the mosquitoes could not get down to the water to drink. Farmers were encouraged to sink artesian wells for irrigation and water power, and cities were urged to sink wells to supply their needs. Rainmakers and their promises to produce needed moisture proliferated throughout the plains states. Then came the "toad stranglers," the rains in the spring of 1892.

The spring of 1892 was exceptionally wet in South Dakota. Rain and snow fell for days on end. Mud was knee deep on the prairie, railroad embankments were washed out, roads – according to the Hand County *Press* of Miller – "had the appearance of a vast bed of mortar" and were impassable.

Samuel W. Glenn, director of the state weather service, reported in Bulletin Number 7 the weather for the period ending May 21. Between January and May over ten inches of moisture had fallen in the Huron area. More than three inches of rain fell in the first twelve days of May, an inch on May 11-12 alone. The weather was continuously cloudy, rainy, and cool. The sun had not shown continuously for an hour in the previous two weeks.

During the week of May 21, the state east of the Missouri River again sustained heavy rains, which were of cloudburst proportions in many places. Fields were flooded and badly washed. During the day of May 21, a strong northerly wind prevailed, driving rain, snow, and sleet across the flooded prairies. Temperatures were near the freezing mark.

The Hand County *Press* for May 26 described the weather during the spring of 1892 as the worst in the history of Hand County. There had been fewer days of sunshine during the first five months of the year than at any other time on record. Trees, grass, and crops showed spring to be at least a month later than usual. On May 20 the area had been visited by an all-day snowstorm. The same conditions prevailed across the border in North Dakota. Cyclone cellars in Miller were caving in from the excessive moisture.

The Blunt *Advocate* in its issue of May 20, 1892, quoted national weather bureau statistics to the effect that the rainfall in the spring of 1892 in the Dakotas was the heaviest in thirty years. A week earlier, the paper had summarized weather conditions with the words, "The total eclipse of the sun still continues." Both Pierre and Huron sustained cloudbursts on May 26 that did extensive damage to streets and buildings. Huron was flooded. Basements were full of water, and the foundation of the Congregational church was sinking.

The Yankton *Press and Dakotan* in its issue of May 18 calculated that flood damage in the state would exceed that of any other year on record. Rail connections out of Sioux Falls had been cut off by high water. Two days later, the paper noted that Frank Zienert had returned to Yankton from Madison. Woonsocket to Scotland, he said, was one vast lake. Snow, high winds, and freezing temperatures made heavy overcoats an absolute necessity. Brookings received its heaviest rainfall on record on May 17. Water on lower Main Street was two to four feet deep and the lower portions of the city were completely under water. Dewing's livery barn was carried off its foundation by the high water.

Sioux City was flooded on May 18, and Yankton was surrounded by water. Having given up hope of ever reaching the boundary by going overland, Bates (no doubt with tongue in cheek) told the Yankton *Press and Dakotan* on May 18 that he had disposed of his horses and wagons and was having flatboats built in which to make the trip from Yankton to Pierre. Two days later, on May 20, snow and freezing temperatures led the Yankton paper to speculate that Bates would have to sell his flatboats and contract for sledges and snowshoes with which to make the trip to Pierre.

Rainfall was so heavy during the spring of 1892 that the stock of the Hand County Rainmakers' Association was watered down to the point where it was worth no more than four cents on the dollar. On May 12 – it rained every day in Miller between May 12-19 – the Hand County *Press* carried a plaintive advertisement reading: "Lost, strayed, or stolen – a sentiment known to exist in this community once, and crystalized under the name of 'Rainmakers Association.' If found adrift, a suitable reward will be paid for its anchorage."

Before the heavy rains of May, a rainmaking experiment had been slated for

General Robert G. Dyrenforth conducted rain-making experiments in Texas during the drought of the 1890s. He used dynamite and oxy-hydrogen ballons.

Another type of rain-making device which was used in Nebraska.

Rain-making devices used during the drought of the 1890s.

Doland in Spink County. The trial was to be conducted by the Kansas Experimental Rain Company, with A. B. Montgomery in charge. According to the Aberdeen *Daily News* on April 20, Montgomery was so confident that he could make it rain at his pleasure that he had asked only for a date to be set and he would be at Doland to make it "pour."

Because April had been so wet, those in charge thought it best to postpone the test until late May – when a good rain would be appreciated. Accordingly, the date was set for May 20. The scheduled experiment aroused a great deal of interest. The Mandan *Pioneer* carried the announcement on May 20 that special trains would be run, offering reduced rates, for the accommodation of those who wanted to be on hand to see the test.

When May proved to be even wetter than April, the Blunt *Advocate* advised on May 13 that the authorities should prevent the test; otherwise, it warned, people would have to leave the country in boats. The rainmakers later postponed their experiment at Doland to June 27, but they promised that if the rain continued, they could dispel the clouds as well as make them.

The rainmakers at Doland in 1892 fared better than one who offered his services to farmers around Minden, Nebraska, that year. Having failed to make good his claims, the rainmaker departed from the farming community soaking wet, but not from any moisture that he had coaxed into the area. Farmers, disgruntled over his failure to reverse the dry spell, had tied him to a telegraph pole and doused him with water from the town's firehose.

Needing neither snowshoes nor flatboats, a part of Bates' crew – Charles Wright, Harry Wright, George W. Osborn, Charles Campbell, and C. R. Wheeler – left Yankton with horses and wagons on May 23, bound for Miller. Other crew members from Pierre joined them there. Bates left Yankton for Miller by train on May 30, Decoration Day.

The same day, according to the Hand County *Press,* Bates and his crew passed through Miller on their way to the point at which the Missouri River crossed the state boundary. If he intended to use the ferry at Winona to get his men and equipment across the river, Bates may have experienced difficulty. Because of an outbreak of diphtheria, Winona was placed under quarantine on May 26 and all traffic by ferry across the river was halted. The quarantine was still not lifted by June 2, according to the Winona paper. On June 1 high waves driven by a strong south wind made it impossible to get the mail from Winona to Fort Yates.

In his field notes, Bates recorded June 6 as the date on which he commenced work on the seventh standard parallel in 1892. On the previous day, he took the preliminary oaths of his assistants: George W. Osborn, C. R. Wheeler, Charles Wright, and H. M. Finotti, chainmen and stonesetters; G. W. Theim, Harry Wright, Ira Griggs, Theodore Jackson, Joe Patterson, Fred C. Clemons, Ernest Muchler, Anton Naadeu, Charles Campbell, and George Wolf, teamsters and stonesetters; and William Jones and C. H. Armstrong, flagmen and stonesetters.

Bates' instruments were those he had used in 1891: an engineer's transit with a solar attachment. The transit was in perfect adjustment at the time he commenced the work, and he frequently tested it during the 1892 season and kept it in perfect adjustment. Chaining, as in 1891, was done with two steel tapes adjusted to a length of sixty-six feet from a standard tape that had been adjusted at the surveyor general's office at Huron, South Dakota. Both tapes were frequently checked during the season to assure their accuracy.

As was suggested to him in the supplemental special instructions dated March 23, 1892, Bates employed the method of setting the parallel from a "secant line through four mile points on the parallel." Bates would write later that after many years of experience running parallels by the tangent principle with its long offsets and the labor of turning azimuths, he could not "too highly commend the process by the secant line; securing thereby greater accuracy and convenience in establishing the parallel, and noting topography thereon." Frequent tests in the field had convinced Bates that using the secant method was both convenient and accurate.

It was not difficult for Bates to begin his work on the seventh standard parallel in 1892 because he had already set mile monument 190 the previous November. Arriving at the monument and corner to township 129 north, ranges 78 and 79 west, fifth principal meridian in latitude 45° 55′ 20″ N., he set up his equipment and prepared to measure the distance across the Missouri River by triangulation.

On June 6 at 2:19 a.m., Bates observed Polaris in its most eastern elongation so that he might turn off an azimuth to the west. From the line so obtained, he started the secant line west according to his instructions dated March 23, 1892. Running through dense brush, he reached the left bank of the river, which was twelve feet high and being undercut by the force of the rushing water.

Bates does not indicate in his field notes how he got his men and equipment across the river, only that he "proceeded across the river" and, following the instructions to use at least "two independent well-conditioned triangles," from the measurements obtained, calculated the distance across the river to be 51.29⅔ chains, the "recorded distance between flags on the secant line." The right bank of the river was five feet high and bearing north and south.

Once on the right bank of the Missouri and having the monuments at hand – he had hired men and teams in the Winona vicinity to haul the monuments – Bates could begin the 1892 surveying season in earnest. The half-mile point between miles 190 and 191 came in the middle of the river, so that half-mile monument was not set. The bottom land on the west side of the Missouri River was covered with a heavy growth of cottonwood timber and dense brush. One-half mile west of the river, on a bench twenty feet above the bottom, Bates came to the village of a chief named "Belly Fat." In the midst of the village, his crew set the monument to mark mile 191. Because Bates was running an original survey, the markings on the monuments were the same as those used on the Sisseton and Wahpeton Indian Reservation.

Monument 190 marked a township corner, so monument 191 bore one groove on its east face and five grooves on its west face to indicate the distances to the preceding and succeeding township corners. The letters "N.D." and "S.C."were on the north face of the monument, and the letters "S.D." were on the south face. The number indicating the mile was on the east face.

From this point, the boundary followed along or near the narrow valley of Blackfoot Creek until it reached the top of the bluffs and moved onto the plateau near mile monument 200, a point 575 feet above the Missouri River. The underbrush thinned out and was replaced by sparse, short vegetation; the land was rolling prairie and the soil was second to third rate sand, clay, or gumbo. To mark mile 196, Bates set the first township corner marker west of the river. At that point, on the night of June 8, he made his first recorded observation after crossing the river of Polaris in its most eastern elongation. From thence, he proceeded west on the secant. At mile 200 the land was hilly and broken with washouts and little badlands. Monument 200 was set on the east slope of a steep hill.

The monument marking mile 202, a township corner, was set, wrote Bates, "in the face of a nearly perpendicular bluff 100 ft. high, and about 40 ft. from the top." Included in Bates' field notes is a photograph of his men setting the monument. Erosion has long since claimed monument 202. It lies today at the base of the bluff on which it was set.

Bates covered the distance from mile 196 to mile 205 between June 8 and June 11, a period that included a trip to Winona. Improving on the instructions that he must take observations on Polaris at elongation once in each stretch of thirty-six miles – he took them about every ten miles – Bates at mile 205 on the night of June 11 observed Polaris, and the next morning he proceeded west on the secant. From here the line followed on or near the summit of the divide between the Cannonball and Grand rivers. The surface was rolling prairie with some stretches of stony hills. At about mile 230, the surface of the country became more broken and hilly, with sandstone-capped hills and knolls. The soil was generally sandy with a fair growth of wild grasses and some cacti. Occasional outcroppings of a very poor grade of lignite were found along prairie drains and in washouts. Water was scarce.

Bates' men setting mile monument 202. South Dakota State Historical Society.

It was at this point that Bates may have had a visit from one of his superiors. The Dickinson *Press* observed that Commissioner Carter of the General Land Office had been in Dickinson on June 21. Carter planned to retire and return to his law practice, according to the *Daily Huronite* for April 30, as soon as he had made his annual report in July. There was some speculation that he might be a candidate for the United States Senate in the fall of 1892. E. A. Wilson, the surveyor general for North Dakota, came to Dickinson from Bismarck on June 23 and went south of town, reported the Dickinson *Press,* "to look after the surveying going on there." It is conceivable that either Carter or Wilson or both intended to examine the survey that Bates was running on the state boundary.

Bates reached mile 246 on July 3. After leaving the Missouri River, he and his crew had covered fifty-five miles in a little more

Looking east toward the "nearly perpendicular bluff 100 ft. high," on the face of which Bates' men set mile monument 202, which lies today at the base of the bluff. Photo by the author.

than three weeks. One-half mile west of mile 246, he crossed the old Bismarck and Deadwood stage road. That night, on the eve of the Fourth of July, Bates took another observation on Polaris. The country through which the crew was passing was unsettled. Bates' field notes for this long stretch of the boundary include no bearings nor distances to objects that had been erected by man.

July 4 was a working day for Bates and his crew, although had they been of a mind to do so they could have taken in the Independence Day celebration in Dickinson. According to the Dickinson *Press,* festivities began at 9:00 a.m. and included a street parade, a Trades' Display, platform exercises ("Orations, Music, Etc., Etc."), a ball game, and horse races. There were also bicycle and foot races. A Grand Ball in the evening ended the day's festivities.

At 7.40 chains west of the monument marking mile 263, Bates intersected the west boundary line of the Standing Rock Indian Reservation, which was 102° west longitude from Greenwich. To mark the point, he deposited two empty fruit cans and set a sandstone monument marked as per his instructions from the General Land Office. Eight links west of the monument, he raised a mound of earth two and one-half feet high and five feet across at the base. The earth was taken from three diamond-shaped pits measuring forty by forty by twelve inches. The land was high and hilly prairie and the soil was third rate sandy loam. Vegetation was fair.

On July 8, when they attempted to set the monument marking mile 276, Bates' men struck a hard sandstone formation at a depth of two and one-half feet, which they could not penetrate. Of the 720 monuments that were set along the length of the boundary, this is the only one that could not be set at its proper depth of three and one-half feet. Setting the monument as deeply as possible, Bates' men raised a mound of earth around it, five feet at the base and three feet high. That night, at monument 278, Bates took another observation on Polaris. The crew had covered twelve miles that day, over "rolling prairie with stony and gravelly ridges." Vegetation varied from good to fair. It would have been about at this point that Bates set the last of the monuments that had been shipped from Pierre to St. Benedict.

A correction had to be made on monument 287. A quarryman had originally marked it "288." From this monument, wrote Bates in his field notes, "Wolf Butte, a double topped, sandstone capped butte, about 250 ft. above the corner, bears S. 47° W. A very prominent land mark." Bates' field notes include a photograph of Wolf Butte, taken from the next half-mile monument. At monument 287, on the night of July 9, Bates took another observation of Polaris. His crew proceeded west on the

Wolf Butte as seen from the half-mile monument between monuments 287 and 288. South Dakota State Historical Society.

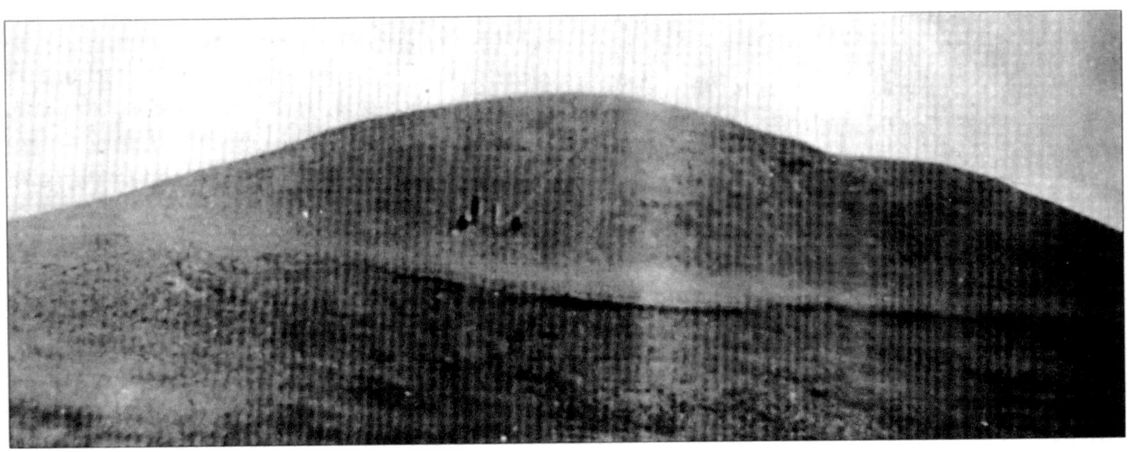

Bates' men setting mile monument 304. South Dakota State Historical Society.

secant the next morning over "high hilly prairie," covered with flint boulders. Vegetation was thin and included cacti.

Bates' crew was covering about ten miles per day. Monument 304, marking a township corner, was set on the afternoon of July 10 on the north slope of a knoll eighty feet high. A photograph included in Bates' field notes shows the men setting the monument. That night, Bates took another observation on Polaris.

At this point, Bates entered the valley of the North Fork of the Grand River, a stream that the crew had to cross many times because it meanders back and forth across the boundary. Between miles 307 and 309, the crew crossed the river ten times. The river varied in width from ten to twenty feet and had banks eight to fifteen feet high. Fortunately, the water was only six inches deep. Bates wrote that the water was brackish and almost unfit for use. The river bottoms contained no timber.

Still in the valley of the North Fork of the Grand River, Bates set monument 310, another township corner. At a point 23.15 chains west of this monument, Bates intersected the meridian which was 103° west longitude from Greenwich. Here, as instructed, he built a closing corner and marked it with an inscribed sandstone monument, a mound of earth, and three pits. Older area residents remember seeing the sandstone monument, but it has now disappeared. The mound and pits have been obliterated by time and the elements.

In mid-July Bates and his men took a break from their labors. They were about seventy miles south of Dickinson, they had been in the field for six weeks, and they welcomed a respite from work. Just west of monument 316, at which Bates took an observation on Polaris on the night of July 11, the parallel intersected the wagon road that ran from Dickinson to the Black Hills. Bates made his next observation at mile 325 on July 27.

The Dickinson *Press* on July 16 reported that Bates had come into town on July 14 for repairs and supplies and had "loaded out" the next day. George Wolf, one of Bates' teamsters and stonesetters, had also been in town. He told the newspaper that "it was quite a treat to get into town for a day" after having been in the field for so long.

Perhaps Bates and his men were entertained while in Dickinson by the Kickapoo Medicine Advertising Company, which had been in town since July 4. The Dickinson *Press* on July 16 described how deserted the streets of Dickinson were each evening from 8:30 to 10:00 – everyone was at the Kickapoo performance. Nothing since the establishment of the town equalled the excitement and interest generated by the troupe.

The company consisted of two performers. Hall, the comedian, was a genius with a large fund of humor. A crayon artist, a "paper manipulator," a Negro impersonator, a "fire king," and a musician who could play a dozen instruments – he was a whole show in himself. Professor Whipple, the magician, had the finest collection of stereopticon views that had ever been exhibited in Dickinson.

But the company provided more than entertainment. It also offered healing. People were invited to visit the doctor at his office on the campgrounds for free consultation and advice at any time. Everyone, declared the Dickinson *Press,* had heard of the successful removal of the tapeworm that had made life a burden for Frank Lish. The Kickapoos had also removed tapeworms from Adam Imhoff and from his wife. In each case, the operation had been "brilliantly successful." Because not one physician in a thousand could remove these parasites and because their attempts to do so never cost less than $100, it could easily be understood why the people of Dickinson felt "the most kindly interest in the success of the Kickapoo Medicine Company."

Returning to the survey, Bates and his men at mile 325 on July 27 again began encountering the North Fork of the Grand River, which they had to cross several times in the next few miles. The river was dry, except for a few holes which contained brackish water. Its banks were usually about twelve feet high. Just before reaching mile 327, the crew crossed the Medora and Black Hills wagon road, bearing north and south. From here to the Montana boundary, the country was a high rolling and hilly prairie, in places very broken and cut with washouts and badlands.

There were no settlers along the boundary west of the Missouri River, but the country west of the Indian reservation was used for grazing thousands of head of cattle. In the vicinity of the Little Missouri, wrote Bates in his field notes, the annual rainfall was so light that the country would not support agriculture. Native grasses did well, however. Cured on the stem, they provided excellent winter grazing on which the cattle thrived without any other feed. About fifty miles south of New England City, along the Grand River in South Dakota, according to one account, the Plum and Clark Ranch ran up to 20,000 head of cattle and horses. Near where the Little Missouri River entered North Dakota, the Hashknife outfit ran 35,000 to 40,000 head. Near the present town of Marmarth the OX ranch was located, and north of there the 777 Ranch at one time ran about 25,000 cattle.

Just west of mile 331, Bates came to the north point of the Cave Hills, a range of high hills bearing north and south with perpendicular stone sides three hundred feet high. The hills were covered with a heavy growth of pines on their tops, which from a distance appeared to be nearly level. Monument 335 was set "in a broad, well beaten cattle trail."

Three miles farther west, at monument 338, on July 28, Bates again observed Polaris in its most eastern elongation. From the monument marking the half mile between miles 342 and 343, Bates took a bearing on the northeast point of the "Pommes Blanches Hills." The hills appeared to be a bluff five hundred to six hundred feet high, facing to the northwest and covered with young timber and brush. The top appeared to be a plateau sloping gently to the south. The men were again making frequent crossings of the North Fork of the Grand River.

Between miles 345 and 346, Bates came to the summit of the divide between the Little Missouri and the Grand rivers. About one mile north of this point, he noted, was located a "black, bare, washed hill or bluff, 60 to 80 feet high." Monument 346 was set at a township corner and here the land remained high rolling prairie. The soil was third rate sand and gumbo. Vegetation was only fair and included some cacti and sagebrush. On August 1, at monument 347, Bates took an observation on Polaris. The men had covered ten miles during the previous three days. One of them was a Sunday. Perhaps the men rested from their labors on the Sabbath. Or perhaps the rough terrain was slowing their progress.

The line now lay through rolling prairie and washouts. The men were approaching the Little Missouri River. As Bates described it, "The country north and south of the line is generally walled with high black bluffs; and the bottoms cut with washouts; numerous clay buttes and mounds; forming a part of the famous bad lands of the Little Missouri river." Later he wrote, "in the vicinity of the Little Missouri river the whole country is broken with badlands of

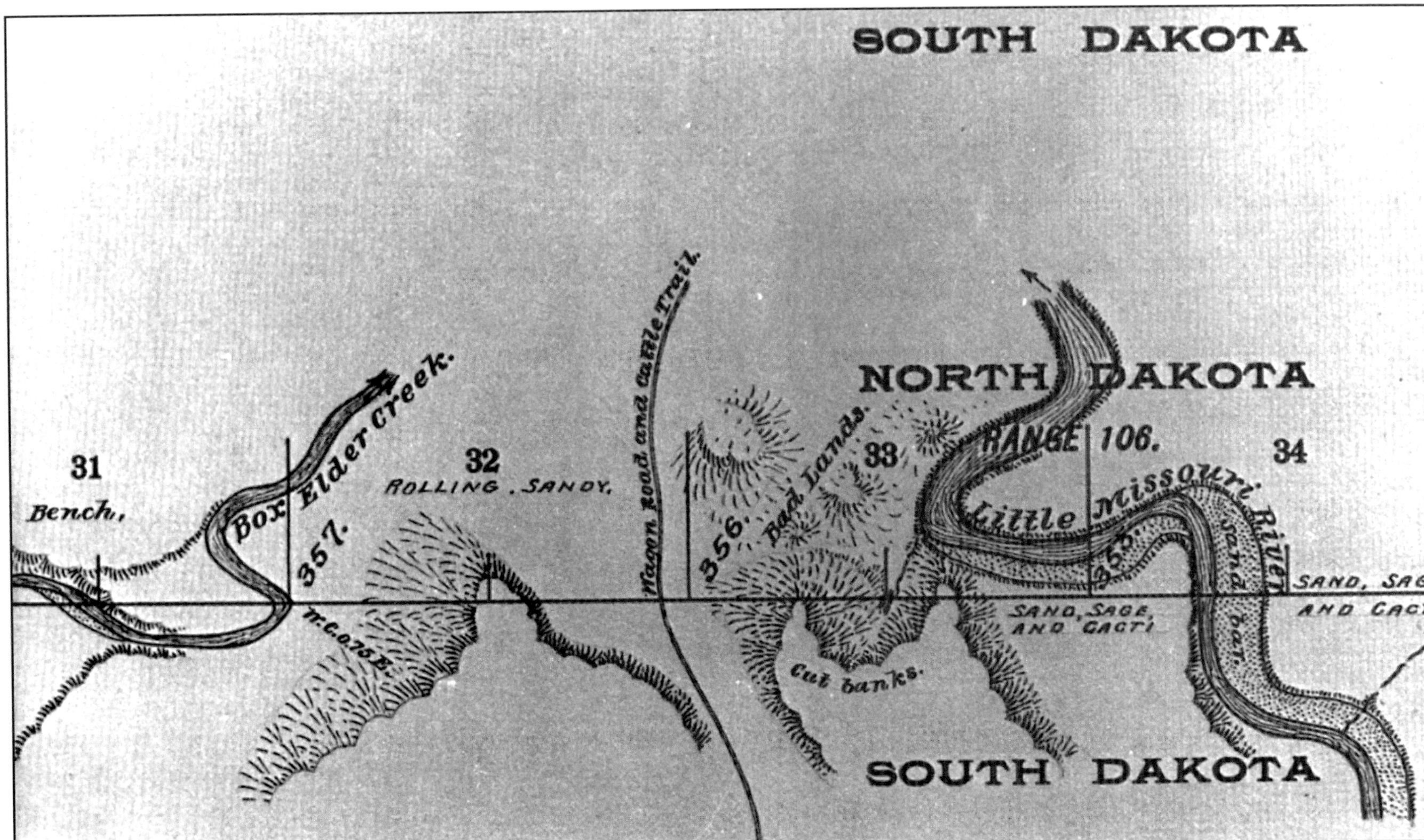

Bates' map of the boundary at its crossing of the Little Missouri River and Box Elder Creek, showing the ruggedness of the terrain. South Dakota State Historical Society.

Badlands of the Little Missouri River, north of the half-mile monument between monuments 355 and 356. South Dakota State Historical Society.

swiftest creeks in the Dakotas. Now occurred only the second instance in setting 720 monuments that Bates could not place the monument in a section corner. "Mile point coming in creek," wrote Bates in his field notes, "where it is impossible to set the monument; at a point 75 lks. E. , and on top of the cut bank, I set a *Witness* 357th mile post and S.C. for secs. 31 and 32. . . . "

That Bates set the witness monument where he did attests to his appreciation for the swiftness of the current and for the volume of water carried by Box Elder Creek. The water ran in a stream eighty feet wide and three feet deep. Bates' precautions

a grand and sublime character. The vegetation is generally thin and short." Just before reaching mile 355, Bates crossed the Little Missouri, the banks of which were twelve to fifteen feet high. The water in the river, which Bates described as "good water," was two chains wide and six inches deep.

Once west of the Little Missouri, with "bad lands in sight on all sides," the men began ascending "high steep washed hills." They were encountering bluffs up to 125 feet high. On a "bare clay point," the men set the monument marking the half mile between miles 355 and 356. Bates included in his field notes a photograph of the Badlands lying north of this monument. Claimed by erosion, the monument lies today at the bottom of a steep bluff, as does a rancher's fence which he, in a vain effort to anchor it, had attached to the monument.

A short distance west of the Little Missouri River, Bates came to Box Elder Creek, which must be one of the largest,

Badlands of the Little Missouri River, north of the half-mile monument between monuments 355 and 356, as they appear today. Many features remain as they were when Bates and his men passed through the area a century ago. Photo by the author.

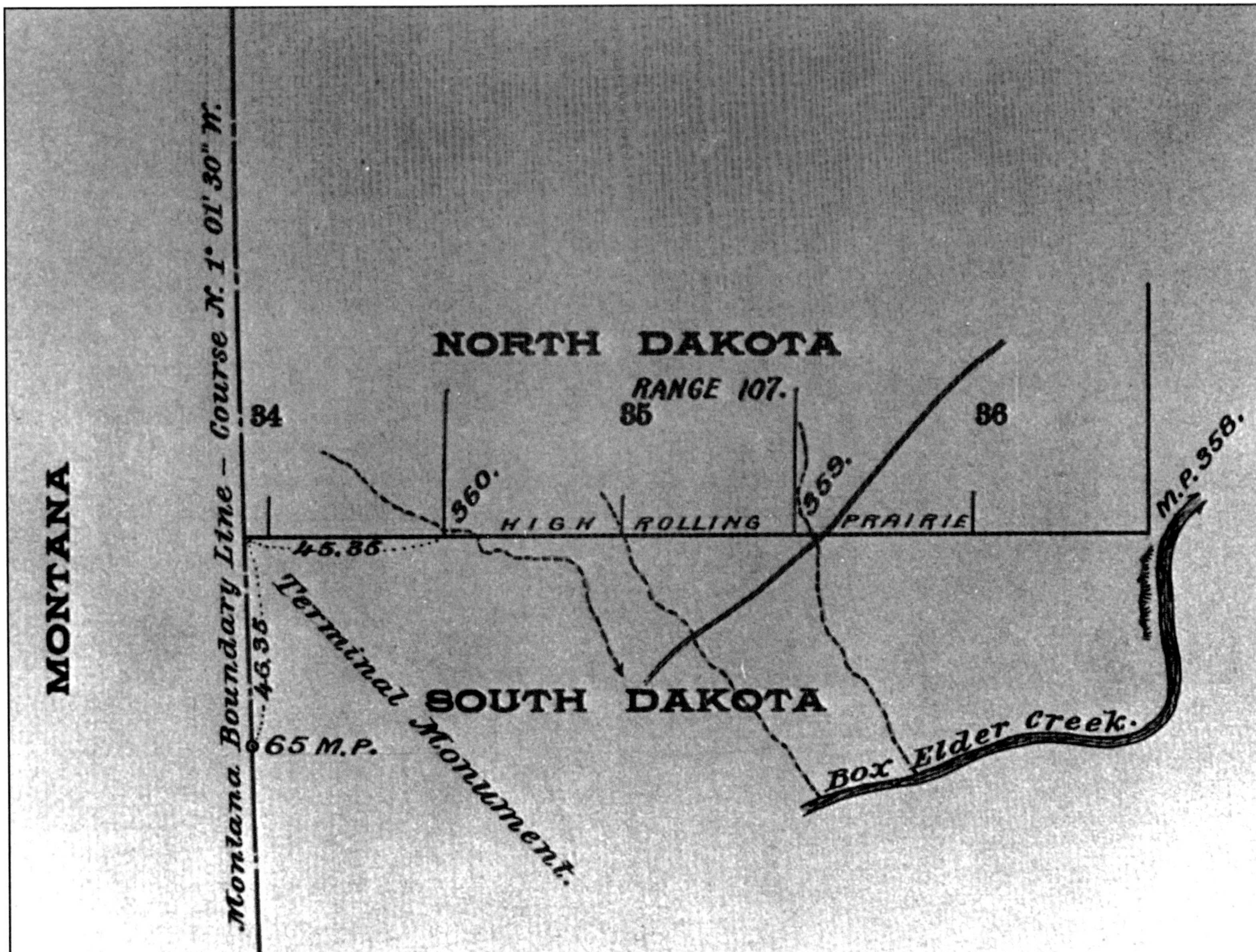

Bates' map of the boundary between Box Elder Creek and the terminal monument, showing the juncture of the North Dakota, South Dakota, and Montana boundaries. South Dakota Historical Society.

were to no avail. Monument 357 has been washed away by the force of Box Elder Creek, one of the few water courses in western North Dakota, thought Bates, that carried water throughout the entire summer.

The date was August 2 and the Montana boundary was little more than three miles to the west. Had it been marked with monuments similar to those the men were setting, they could have seen it. That night, Bates made another observation of Polaris.

For the next mile of the boundary, which Bates ran the next morning, the crew worked in or on the banks of Box Elder Creek in water nearly up to their knees. At 72.43 chains west of monument 357, they came to the foot of a nearly perpendicular bluff sixty feet high. The bluff has been undercut by the creek. Leaving the creek bed and ascending the bluff, the men set monument 358 for the standard corner and for township 129 north, ranges 106 and 107 west.

From his observations and measurements, Bates knew when he had reached the Montana boundary, and the twenty-seventh meridian of longitude west from Washington, D.C., but he could not immediately find any evidence left by surveyors to confirm his calculations. In his field notes for the date of August 4, a hot day – the thermometer reached 104°F in the shade at South Heart· southwest of Dickinson – Bates recounted the difficulties he encountered in locating the exact point at which to set the terminal monument. "After nearly two days search to find the east boundary line of Montana," he wrote, "I found the 65th mile post lying on the ground in a Buffalo wallow. . . . " "The post," concluded Bates, "had undoubtedly been rubbed down by cattle, as thousands of them range over this country."

This was a post that had been set by Daniel G. Major in 1885, when he surveyed the boundary between Montana and Dakota territories. On most of the surveys he ran, Daniel Major was joined by his brother John J. Major, who acted in the capacity of recorder, computer, and assistant surveyor. The Major brothers enjoyed the distinction of having surveyed more state boundary lines than any other surveyors in the country. The cottonwood post was five inches square and four feet long, marked, wrote Bates, "27° W. L. on the N., 65 M. on the S. , D. on the E., and M. on the W., with a marked stone and a tin can at the foot. . . . "

The "65th mile post" to which Bates referred had been set sixty-five miles north of the intersection of the Wyoming, Montana, and South Dakota boundaries, a point which lies on the forty-fifth parallel of north latitude. Bates also found some pits and traces of a mound. He set the post in place and measured north eighty chains, where he made a careful, but futile, search for the sixty-sixth mile post or mound of Major's survey. Bates found nothing to indicate that the post had ever been set or the mound ever built. He did, however, find, east of a small mound of dirt and stone, a small stone marked "67 M," for mile 67.

From this point, Bates calculated a course and ran back to the sixty-fifth mile post. He then made a careful search for posts, stones, pits, or mounds marking the sixty-third and sixty-fourth miles, but found nothing. Bates ran a line north from the sixty-fifth mile post and found that the line

The terminal monument, marking the juncture of the North Dakota, South Dakota, and Montana boundaries, set in August 1892. The distance from the initial monument on the Minnesota border is 360 miles, 45.35 chains. Photo by the author.

from the south intersected with the one from the east at sixty-five miles plus 48.35 chains, which point was 45.35 chains west from monument 360. At the point of intersection of the lines, Bates set the terminal monument, marked as he had been instructed. Included in Bates' field notes are two photographs of him and an assistant standing by the terminal monument.

From the terminal monument, wrote Bates, he could see, far to the south, a range of pine-timbered hills, which he took to be

Bates (on the left) and one of his men at the terminal monument. South Dakota State Historical Society.

the Long Pine and Short Pine Hills. Also at the terminal monument, observed Bates, the eastern boundary of Montana appeared to be "badly out of course, and nearly obliterated." Those pits and mounds that had been dug or built were apparently small originally, and they had been almost completely destroyed by cattle and the elements. Where posts had been set, "the range cattle have undoubtedly rubbed them down. (A circumstance not liable to happen to the posts between N. & S. Dakota)."

United States surveyor Charles H. Bates arrived back in Sturgis, South Dakota, on Monday August 22, 1892, having completed one of the most remarkable surveys in the history of the United States. Charles C. Moody, publisher of the Sturgis *Weekly Record,* scooped every newspaper in the country by being the first to report the exact length of the boundary between North and South Dakota. The boundary, as measured by Bates, was 360 miles, 45.35 chains in length.

Charles C. Moody, publisher of the Sturgis Weekly Record, *who scooped every newspaper in the country by being the first to publish the exact length of the boundary between North and South Dakota.* Deluxe Supplement to the History of Dakota Territory and South Dakota.

The Sturgis *Weekly Record* for August 26, 1892, reported that Bates intended to apply immediately for membership in the Humane Society of the United States. His claim for admission, Bates said, was based on the fact that he had just set 720 "of the most superb scratching posts for cattle that were ever seen." And Bates could attest to

The sharp hooves of livestock have hollowed out a depression around this monument, one of Bates' "superb scratching posts for cattle." Photo by the author.

the monuments' being used for that purpose. He had visited several monuments a few days after they had been set and observed that "they were rubbed smooth by the numerous herds [of cattle] that had been driven into that vicinity. Fertilizer is about a foot deep around every stone. The cattle hold conventions, and love-feasts and picnics and independent rallies around each one."

Chapter 7

Examination of the Survey

"The most perfect and comprehensive boundary line in the United States."
The Steele *Ozone*

Federal regulations, as well as the law of September 25, 1890, providing for surveying and marking the boundary between North and South Dakota, required that a second surveyor examine the survey once Bates had completed it. The cost of the examination would be covered by the money that Congress had appropriated for the project. Of the $25,000 appropriated, Bates received $21,300, leaving $3,700 for the examination.

Senator Pettigrew continued to believe that Bates, with the help of Joe Bailey, had secured his contract by "underhanded means, trickery, and fraud," and he wanted to compel Bates to fulfill the contract to the letter, even if he lost money by doing so. The means at Pettigrew's hand was the requirement that Bates' work had to be examined and approved before he could be paid, and George G. Beardsley of McCanna, North Dakota, was the surveyor in whom the senator placed his confidence. "I know of no man in either state," wrote Pettigrew to Beardsley on September 3, 1891, "who would know better when the work was well done or who would attend to it more efficient [*sic*] than you."

Pettigrew counted Beardsley among his friends and was pleased to have the opportunity to show his appreciation for the friendship by recommending him for the task of examining Bates' work. Pettigrew also asked Henry C. Hansbrough, a steadfast McKenzie man who had been elected North Dakota Senator in 1891, to recommend Beardsley to Thomas H. Carter, the commissioner of the General Land Office.

On September 3, 1891, Carter wrote to the secretary of the interior recommending Beardsley as the examiner and requesting authorization to appoint him. It was incumbent on the General Land Office, wrote Carter, that "great care" be exercised in selecting the person to make the examination of the survey because "upon his report will be based all future action with reference thereto." Both state and federal officials had manifested "considerable anxiety" with reference to the "*proper* establishment" of the boundary, and the Interior Department had frequently in its correspondence expressed the desire that the survey "be executed in a manner compatible with professional excellence. . . . "

Carter also believed it only fair that the United States deputy surveyor chosen to make the required examination be a North Dakotan, because the contract to establish the boundary line had been awarded to a citizen of South Dakota, who in a professional sense could be regarded as a representative of that state.

Commissioner Carter was already acquainted with Beardsley and the quality of his work. During the many years that Beardsley had been professionally connected with the office of the United States surveyor general in Dakota Territory and with the General Land Office, wrote Carter in his September 3 letter, Beardsley had always given "the most complete satisfaction." His contracts for public surveys had all been executed "in a most thorough and satisfactory manner." It also spoke well of Beardsley that, being an experienced surveyor, he had always executed the work "*in his own proper person*. . . . " In his opinion, Carter wrote to the interior secretary, Beardsley possessed "in an eminent degree" all of the qualifications necessary to make a proper examination of Bates' survey.

Major George G. Beardsley, according to his obituary published in the Grand Forks *Daily Herald* on May 21, 1901, was "one of the well known men of the

George G. Beardsley, United States Surveyor who in 1892 examined Charles H. Bates' survey and marking of the North Dakota-South Dakota boundary. State Historical Society of North Dakota.

northwest. . . ." Born in Ohio in 1842, Beardsley had educated himself to be a teacher and while teaching he had trained to become a United States surveyor. Unfortunately, his "very delicate health" (he suffered for many years from tuberculosis and from cirrhosis of the liver) made it difficult for him to secure contracts. He was a surveyor in Minnesota for many years and did a great deal of surveying in the Red River Valley. During the early years of statehood, Beardsley was active in North Dakota politics and he represented Grand Forks County in the first state legislature. In the early 1890s, he purchased a farm at McCanna, one of the many fine farms he owned, and until his death he devoted his attention to farming. Beardsley died in his room at the Prescott Hotel in Grand Forks on May 20, 1901, a few weeks after moving from the Dakotah Hotel, where he usually lived. He had never married and was survived by three sisters and one brother.

It may have been Beardsley's surveying work in Minnesota and in the Red River Valley that brought him to the attention of the Northern Pacific Railroad, for which he rendered a service in June 1871. When the Northern Pacific, building west from Duluth, Minnesota, finally decided where the line would cross the Red River, the company wanted to secure the land for the crossing quietly and cheaply, before speculators obtained it. Beardsley was a principal in the scheme.

In 1870, according to Clement A. Lounsberry's *History of North Dakota*, Thomas H. Canfield of the Lake Superior and Puget Sound Company, a townsite company auxiliary to the Northern Pacific, located the Red River crossing at what became Fargo, North Dakota. For months, rumors had been flying about as speculators and others tried to anticipate where the crossing would be made so that they might locate there and take advantage of the rise in land prices. In 1869 it had been the intention of the Northern Pacific directors to cross the river at or near what is now Grandin. In accordance with that plan, the location of a bridge across the Red River was staked at Elm River, or Grandin, and a settlement of townsite speculators grew up at that point. When the plan was changed in the spring of 1870, a fake line was staked to a point near Moorhead, Minnesota, known as Oakport. Here another village of temporary structures sprang up.

When the location of the crossing was definitely decided upon, the company sent a Mr. Andrew Holes to Alexandria, Minnesota, where he purchased the land for the Moorhead townsite from its owner, Joab B. Smith. The land at Moorhead had been deeded by the Indians, and Smith had entered on the land under the terms of the Pre-emption Act. It remained to secure title to the townsite on the west side of the river.

In 1871 a land office was opened at Pembina, and settlers were expected to rush in to claim the good land of the Red River Valley as soon as the Indian title to the land was extinguished. Some settlers had gone ahead of the surveys and a few had located at what became Fargo. The land at Fargo was not yet open to entry because the Indian title was not extinguished until 1872, but Canfield's townsite company attempted to enter the land by scrip.

Anyone locating on lands west of the Red River at the crossing site had to make "improvements" on it, that is, plow a half acre on each quarter section. Aided by Beardsley, Canfield secured the necessary farm equipment and hid it until Holes returned from Alexandria with the deed to the land for the Moorhead townsite. Then by moonlight on a fine night in June 1871 – sources differ as to the date – Beardsley plowed the necessary land on each of the several quarter sections of land that the townsite company intended to scrip. James B. Power, soon to become the land commissioner for the Northern Pacific, was sent to Pembina to make the scrip locations for the townsite.

On June 29, according to the federal writer's project history of North Dakota, Jacob Lowell, Jr., who with others had been patrolling the Red River since April to discover any indications of the crossing, came on a "Farmer Brown" who, with three Scandinavian settlers, was squatting on what became the Fargo townsite. Although Farmer Brown was wearing well-worn overalls, a brown hat, and a hickory shirt and "leaned with grace and ease upon the handles of his plow," Lowell doubted that he was a farmer. About "Farmer Brown,"according to Erling N. Rolfsrud in his book *The Story of North Dakota,* the suspicious Lowell made these comments: "[He] talked learnedly and interestingly of pumpkins and corn, and of the great capacity of Red River soil for wheat. No, he had never raised townsites and really did not know when was the best season for planting them." Lowell and his associates located on land near "Brown" on July 1 and 2, 1871.

When it was discovered that Farmer Brown was really Beardsley and that he was in the employ of the townsite company, a rush of settlers followed. Some of them located on the land the townsite company intended to scrip. Because Beardsley and his party were in the employ of the Lake Superior and Puget Sound Company and could not be considered bona fide settlers, their prior occupancy was contested. After much litigation, the Lake Superior and Puget Sound Company withdrew its claim to the land at the Fargo townsite, leaving the contestants in possession of the even-numbered sections. The Northern Pacific had title to the odd-numbered sections under the terms of its land grant.

Twenty years after his impersonation of a farmer at the Fargo townsite, Beardsley, still a surveyor, was engaged in examining the surveying and marking of the boundary between North and South Dakota. Bates could not be paid for the survey and marking he had completed east of the Missouri River in 1891 until his work had been examined and accepted. His impatience and anxiety at the repeated delays to have the examination undertaken were revealed in his frequent correspondence with the General Land Office.

The General Land Office had assured Bates that the examination of his work would begin in April 1892, but by that date the Interior Department had still not awarded the contract for the examination. Not until July 13, by which time Bates had surveyed and marked the boundary west of the river to a point just south of Dickinson, did the secretary of the interior approve the contract for the examination of the entire boundary from its initial point to the Montana line.

Besides the leisureliness with which Washington seemed to act on such matters, two other issues delayed the awarding of the contract. Beardsley, who was the surveyor favored to receive the contract, was reluctant to undertake the work until he knew for certain what the extent of his responsibilities would be. References to the examiner's responsibilities were vague and consisted of such indefinite phrases as "an examination in the field of the boundary line between the States of North Dakota and South Dakota, as established by Charles H. Bates, U.S. Surveyor, under his contract dated June 4, 1891." Nor could Beardsley, the Interior Department, and the General Land Office agree on the amount by which Beardsley would be compensated for his work. The sum of $3,700 of the original $25,000 appropriation remained, but the Interior Department appeared to want to conserve as much of the $3,700 as possible.

Not until January 23 did Commissioner Carter inform Beardsley, and then only "in a general way," what his duties as the examiner of Bates' work would be, should he be awarded the contract. The examiner would be required "to carefully measure 2 miles of the line (not necessarily contiguous), on every stretch of 6 miles between standard township corners, and to excavate on the E. or W. side of one monument in each distance of 6 miles, to the bottom of a stone mile or 1/2 mile post (as may be most convenient), and to measure the length of the post so exposed."

The examiner would also be required to give a full description of every monument, including its measurements, the distance that it protruded above the ground, the kind of stone from which it was made, and the markings that it bore. Because the markings had to be of sufficient quality to retain their legibility indefinitely, the examiner would have to give a detailed description of them – their size, the depth to which they had been cut, and the neatness with which they had been placed on the monument.

Where the examiner found the distances between the monuments "to exceed or fall short of the standard length of 40 or 80 chains, by an unusual amount," he was to remeasure them as many times as he deemed necessary so that he could testify under oath as to the *"correctness of his own measurements."* The topography along the line was to be noted, as was usual when surveying standard parallels, and bearing trees, if any were found, were to be described. Any blazing through timber also had to be noted. Where Bates had excavated pits or built mounds, the examiner had to note and describe them.

For directions of parts of the line examined, a solar apparatus of approved construction and in perfect adjustment could be used, or azimuths and bearings could be deflected from a true meridian determined by observations on Polaris. A magnetic needle could not be used and no references to variations were to appear in the field notes.

The General Land Office would furnish the examiner who was awarded the contract with the requirements and special instructions under which Bates had completed the survey, as well as with illustrations and descriptions of the marks that were supposed to be placed on the monuments. Because the monuments were "unusually large and conspicuous" and because the line could be easily recognized and followed, the examiner would not be furnished with copies of Bates' field notes and maps.

The figures of $10 and $22 per day had been suggested to Beardsley, from which he would have to pay all the expenses of himself and his crew. He refused to accept the contract under those terms and asked both Senators Pettigrew and Hansborough to intercede with the Interior Department on his behalf to get the amount of compensation increased. On December 16, 1891, Pettigrew wrote to Beardsley, expressing his disappointment that he would not undertake the examination, although he agreed that a compensation of $22 per day

North Dakota Geological Survey camp, showing tent and equipment similar to what Bates and Beardsley and their survey crews would have used. North Dakota Quarterly, *Spring 1970.*

was insufficient. Pettigrew confessed to being "quite astonished" at what seemed to be the niggardliness of the secretary of the interior and promised Beardsley that he would ask the secretary to let the contract for $54 per day,a figure that Beardsley had suggested was the minimum he needed for the work and an amount that Pettigrew did not think was excessive.

On November 5 Beardsley had sent to Commissioner Carter at the General Land Office an itemized estimate of the total daily expenses that he would incur if he undertook the examination of Bates' work. He considered the estimate a reasonable one, considering that he would furnish the labor, the tents, the camp outfit, and the surveying instruments. A reproduction of his estimate is instructive of the costs involved in field surveys conducted during this period:

3 two-horse teams, with covered wagons (for provisions,fuel, camp equipment, etc.)	$5.00	$15.00
1 saddle or buggy horse	2.00	2.00
subsistence for 7 horses	1.00	7.00
2 teamsters	1.50	3.00
1 cook (who was also a teamster)	2.00	2.00
1 chief assistant	5.00	5.00
2 assistants (for testing measurements, course of line)	1.50	3.00
1 chief examiner (Beardsley)	10.00	10.00
subsistence for seven men	1.00	7.00
Total daily expense		$54.00

North Dakota Geological Survey camp kitchen, similar to what Bates and Beardsley and their survey camps would have used. North Dakota Quarterly, *Spring 1970.*

In his letter accompanying the estimate, Beardsley assured Carter that he would complete his examination of Bates' work between the initial point and the Missouri River in thirty days and that the total cost to the federal government would not exceed $1,620. Because Bates had not yet completed his work on the boundary west of the river, Beardsley preferred not to commit himself to a figure for examining this portion of the work until he knew what the examination would entail.

In a letter to the secretary of the interior dated March 22, 1892, Carter wrote that after receiving Beardsley's estimate of his total daily expenses he had given the matter "careful attention" and had concluded that the figure of $54 per day was "*not* disproportionate to the work to be executed and the interests involved." He had also consulted with the United States surveyor general for South Dakota regarding Beardsley's estimate and had been assured that the estimate "was not in any degree exorbitant."

Convinced that Beardsley's figures were fair and reasonable, Carter asked the secretary of the interior for authority to appoint Beardsley as "Special Examiner" to inspect that portion of the boundary between the initial point and the Missouri River. The inspection was to be completed within thirty days after Beardsley's receipt of instructions from the General Land Office, and the total cost of the examination was not to exceed $1,620.

At this point, perhaps eager to have the matter settled and the contract let, Carter suggested to Beardsley that he submit a figure for which he would inspect the entire line of the survey between the states, both east and west of the Missouri River. Beardsley obliged and on April 13 submitted a second proposition. He now offered to examine the survey of the entire boundary for a sum not to exceed $3,240, thus leaving a remainder of $460 of the original appropriation of $25,000.

On April 22 Carter recommended to Secretary of the Interior John W. Noble that Beardsley's proposition be accepted and that he be appointed to examine Bates' survey and marking of the boundary. Noble accepted Carter's recommendation and on May 6 authorized him to enter into a contract with Beardsley. Carter informed Beardsley on May 18 of Noble's decision and included in his letter triplicate forms of a contract and of a bond, which Beardsley was to complete and return to the General Land Office. By this date, Bates was nearly ready to leave Yankton and take to the field for the start of the 1892 surveying season. He still had no word as to the examination of his work, nor had he been paid for any of it. The financial lot, at least, of a United States surveyor was indeed not a happy one.

Under cover of a letter dated May 31, 1892, Beardsley sent to Carter's office triplicate copies of the contract and his bond as "examiner of the Boundary line survey between the States of North Dakota and South Dakota. . . . " By the terms of the contract, Beardsley promised that he would "well, truly, and faithfully examine the survey of the boundary line between the States of North Dakota and South Dakota, as executed by Charles H. Bates, U.S. Surveyor. . . . " He would perform his duties "in strict conformity with the laws of the United States, the printed manual of surveying instructions, approved December 2, 1889, and other surveying instructions issued by the Commissioner of the General Land Office and with such special instructions" as the commissioner might issue.

On penalty of forfeiture of $6,480, double the amount of the compensation he was to receive, Beardsley promised to complete the examination of the survey of that part of the boundary line lying east of the Missouri River and return his report within three months of May 27, which was the date on which he had signed the contract. He would complete the examination of the survey of that part of the boundary lying west of the Missouri River and return his report within three months from the date he received special instructions pertaining to this portion of the boundary.

Beardsley also promised that "no member of or delegate to Congress or subcontractor" would be entitled to any share of the compensation, nor would any of the examination be executed by anyone other than himself "in his own proper person." The contract also stipulated that Beardsley could not begin the examination until he had been officially notified that the secretary of the interior had approved the contract. Judge Robert M. Carothers of Grand Forks, United States circuit court commissioner for the district of North Dakota, examined and certified Beardsley's bond, with Michael L. McCormack and Frank Viets as sureties.

And now occurred what for both Beardsley and Bates was another vexing delay. On June 14 William M. Stone, who was acting commissioner in Carter's absence, wrote to Beardsley. Carter was not in Washington and was not expected to return until the end of June. On June 21, the Dickinson *Press* reported, Carter was in Dickinson, possibly on his way to Montana. Because he was one of the parties to the contract, together with Beardsley, Carter's signature was required before the contract could be executed and submitted to the secretary of the interior for his approval.

Not until July 13, 1892, did the secretary of the interior approve the contract between Beardsley and Commissioner Carter for the General Land Office. Beardsley was informed of the secretary's action by letter on July 25, and, as stipulated in the contract, he was not allowed to begin the examination until he had received this notification. The tardiness with which Beardsley's contract with the General Land Office had been executed and approved created difficulties for both of the two United States surveyors who were affected by the contract.

On July 25 – he was now less than forty miles from the Montana boundary – Bates wrote yet another time to Commissioner Carter regarding his compensation for the work he had done in 1891. "The work west of the river is fast drawing to a close," wrote Bates, and he had not yet heard whether an examiner had been appointed, when the examination would be undertaken, nor when he might expect to be compensated for the work completed during the previous season.

The "urgency" for the money was "very great" and causing him "a great deal of anxiety," wrote Bates, because when he had finished the survey to the Montana line he would discharge the members of his crew and they would have to be paid. Bates also had to meet other expenses incurred in the course of conducting the survey. Bates' anxieties were little quieted beyond being informed by Acting Commissioner Stone on August 5 that Beardsley had been instructed both by telegram and by letter "to report on that part of the boundary east of the Missouri River at earliest date."

For Beardsley the delay meant that, under the terms of his contract, he might be required to forfeit his bond. Beardsley had agreed to make the examination of the boundary line and submit his report within three months from May 27, 1892, the date of his contract. When he entered into the contract, he wrote to Carter on July 29, he assumed the contract would be approved "in about the time it usually takes to have an ordinary surveying contract . . . approved." Beardsley "had no idea" it would take over two months to approve the contract; otherwise he would not have entered into it.

Less than one month remained of the three months allowed Beardsley to make the examination and submit his final report. He could not possibly do the work in that time. Consequently, he asked Carter for an extension of three months from July 29, the date of his letter, or from July 25, the date he was officially notified that his contract and bond had been approved. Beardsley informed Carter that he would begin the examination as soon as he could reach the boundary. He was in Fargo at the time of his writing, and he requested Carter to contact him there by telegraph.

Beardsley's request was granted. By telegram on July 30 and in letters on August 3 and 5, Acting Commissioner Stone informed Beardsley that the time for the examination and reporting had been extended for three months from August 1, namely, until October 31, 1892. Beardsley was instructed to begin the examination at the initial point and proceed west to the Missouri River, reporting on that portion of the boundary at the earliest possible date. The western portion of the boundary could be reported on, as stipulated, within three months from the receipt of special instructions.

His contract approved and an extension for reporting granted, Beardsley proceeded to the examination with dispatch. On September 1, 1892, the Winona *Times* reported that Beardsley had been in Winona the week before, having completed the examination of the boundary from the initial point to the Missouri River. Beardsley's crew had apparently crossed the Missouri River on the ferry between Winona and Fort Yates and were then at work examining Bates' survey on the west side of the river.

On September 21 Beardsley came into Dickinson from the south, having completed the examination of the state line from the initial point to the Montana boundary. Bates' work, declared Beardsley to the Dickinson *Press,* was "a marvel of accuracy." From Dickinson, Beardsley traveled cross country to Grand Forks, and local newspapers in towns through which he passed published accounts of Bates' work and Beardsley's examination of it. The Bismarck *Settler*—Beardsley was delayed for a time at Mandan "on account of ferriage" over the Missouri River—reported that the monuments on the boundary were all "uniform and nicely set." Under the heading "The Line Between the Dakotas Held Down by Granite Blocks," the Steele *Ozone* on October 8, 1892, described the border Beardsley had examined as "the most perfect and comprehensive boundary line in the United States."

In July Beardsley had requested and had been granted an extension to October 31, 1892, for submitting his report on the examination. On November 5, 1892, he was forced by ill health to request another extension, this one to January 1, 1893. According to his physician, who attested to Beardsley's illness in an affadavit to the commissioner of the General Land Office, Beardsley was unable to perform any mental or physical work because he was suffering from an attack of "nervous prostration," brought on by fatigue and aggravated by his anxiety lest he have to forfeit his bond. The General Land Office granted the extension to January 1, 1893, and Stone so informed Beardsley by letter on November 10.

On December 26 Beardsley transmitted to the General Land Office the field notes of his examinations of the survey and the establishment of the boundary line between the states of North and South Dakota, but only for that portion east of the Missouri River. Illness had prevented him from transcribing the field notes of his examination of the boundary west of the river. Asking for the commissioner's indulgence yet another time, Beardsley promised to submit his field notes and report for that portion of the examination as soon as possible.

He did so on January 14, 1893. Beardsley's field notes and report, after minor corrections, were subsequently approved by the General Land Office. His work was finished.

According to the terms of his contract, Bates could receive "ninety percent of the proportionate amount" due him once he had completed the survey of that portion of the boundary east of the Missouri River. From Buffalo, South Dakota, on October 9, 1892, Bates wrote that payment of this amount "would be of *great* financial benefit" to him. The General Land Office was in receipt of Bates' original field notes and maps for the boundary east of the river, but had to be assured that the work was acceptable before making even partial payment for it. For this reason, the General Land Office awaited Beardsley's report. Once this was received, Stone assured Bates on October 24, 1892, his request for payment would be acted upon.

On the next day, however, Stone wrote to Bates that he would be paid "ninety percent on account" even though Beardsley's report had not yet been submitted. Stone apparently based his decision to award Bates partial compensation on a letter dated October 18, 1892, in which Beardsley had written:

> I found every monument east of the Missouri in its proper place, the stone uniform in kind, quartzite ("or Sioux Falls granite"). They average at least seven feet in length and ten inches wide, and are in almost every case correctly marked and *well* marked. I would say the surveyor did an honest piece of work.

To what must have been Bates' great relief, Stone wrote that he considered "the above quoted favorable remarks upon the character of your work, sufficient for official action and accordingly hereby accept your survey of the boundary line between North and South Dakota, east of the Missouri River. . . . " The acceptance was subject to such corrections on the ground and in the field notes and maps as would be required when Bates' notes were compared with those of Beardsley. Bates would receive, without any further delay, "ninety per cent of the proportionate amount due for the survey and establishment" of that portion of the boundary east of the Missouri River.

Under pain of forfeiting his bond, the terms of Bates' contract required that he send to the General Land Office by November 1, 1892, the original field notes for that portion of the survey from the Missouri River to the Montana boundary. Pleading the press of work and the necessity of completing other surveying contracts during the 1892 season, Bates in September requested that the date by which he had to submit his field notes and maps be extended to March 1, 1893. His request was granted and he was so informed by letter on September 30, 1892.

On February 26, 1893, Bates forwarded to the General Land Office by Adams Express Company a box containing the original field notes, in triplicate, of his survey of the boundary between North and South Dakota from monument 190 to the east line of Montana. The plats, also in triplicate, were included with the field notes.

In acknowledging the receipt of Bates' field notes by letter on March 20, Acting Commissioner M. M. Rose of the General Land Office paid the surveyor the highest of compliments. "Your field notes and maps," wrote Rose, "seem to have been prepared with more than ordinary care and are practically free from errors."

Errors there were. As could be expected with a survey as extensive and as complex as the one of the seventh standard parallel that served as the boundary between North and South Dakota, Bates' field notes contained some errors and omissions that had to be addressed and corrected. Fortunately, Bates could make all the corrections without having to return to the field and repeat any portion of the survey, although he offered to do so should it be necessary.

When the General Land Office examined Bates' field notes and maps and compared them with Beardsley's report, some clerical errors and omissions requiring corrections were discovered for that portion of the boundary lying east of the Missouri River. Three lists were sent to Bates for his attention. The three copies of the field notes were also returned to Bates so that the corrections could be made in his own handwriting. A "cursory examination" suggested that no corrections would be required in Bates' field notes for that portion of the boundary lying west of monument 190.

List number one was entitled "Changes and Corrections to be Made" and required Bates to make some changes by erasures and corrections and rewrite a few pages of his field notes. List number two, entitled "Errors and Omissions," was longer and dealt with sightings on and distances to topographical features and objects of human construction such as buttes and houses. The third list was entitled "Errors

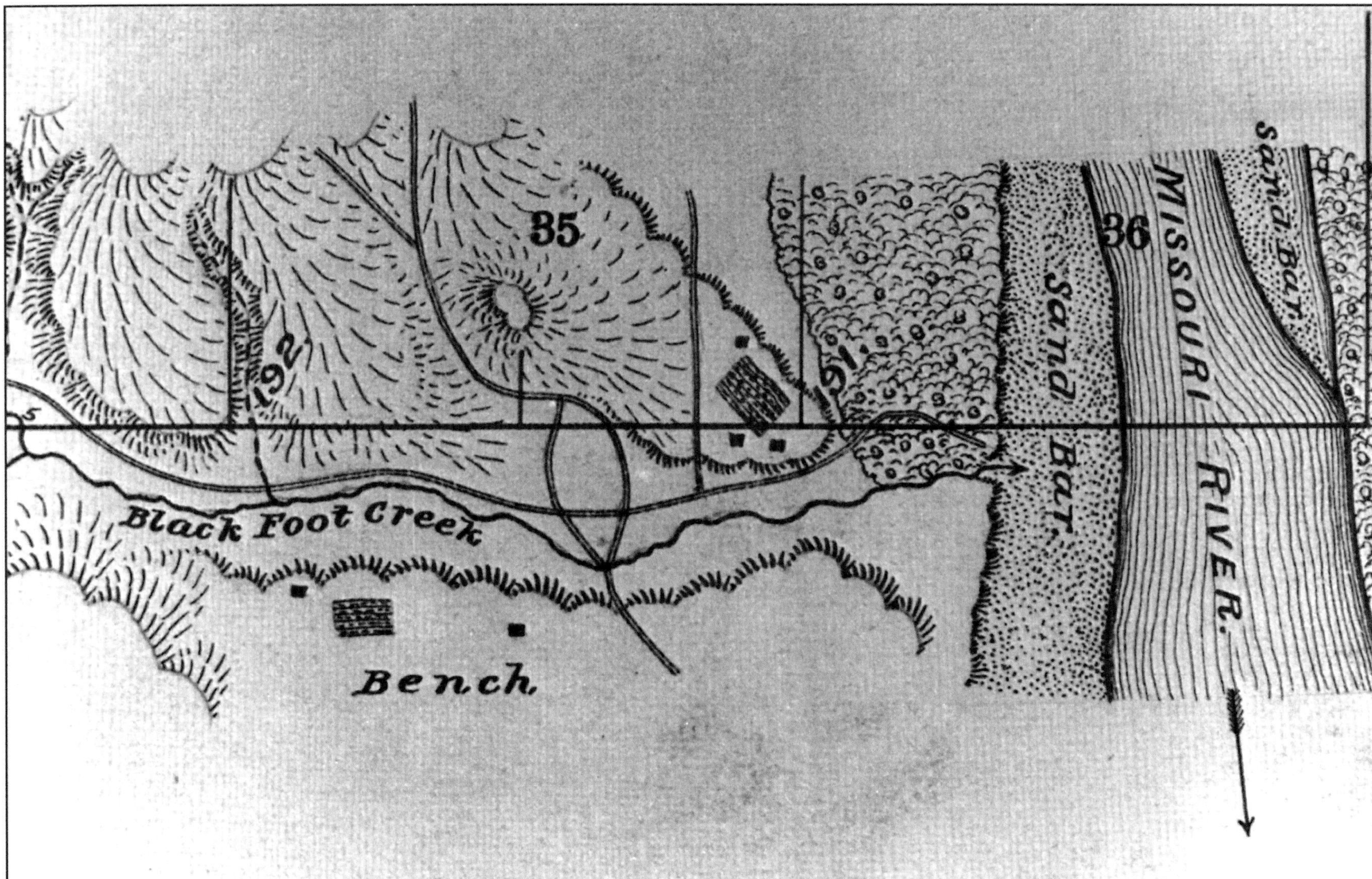

Drawn on the scale of two inches to a mile, this map shows the boundary between mile monuments 190 and 193 and illustrates the detail that Bates had to include on his plats. The small, dark squares and wavy lines at mile monument 191 mark the site of an Indian village. South Dakota State Historical Society.

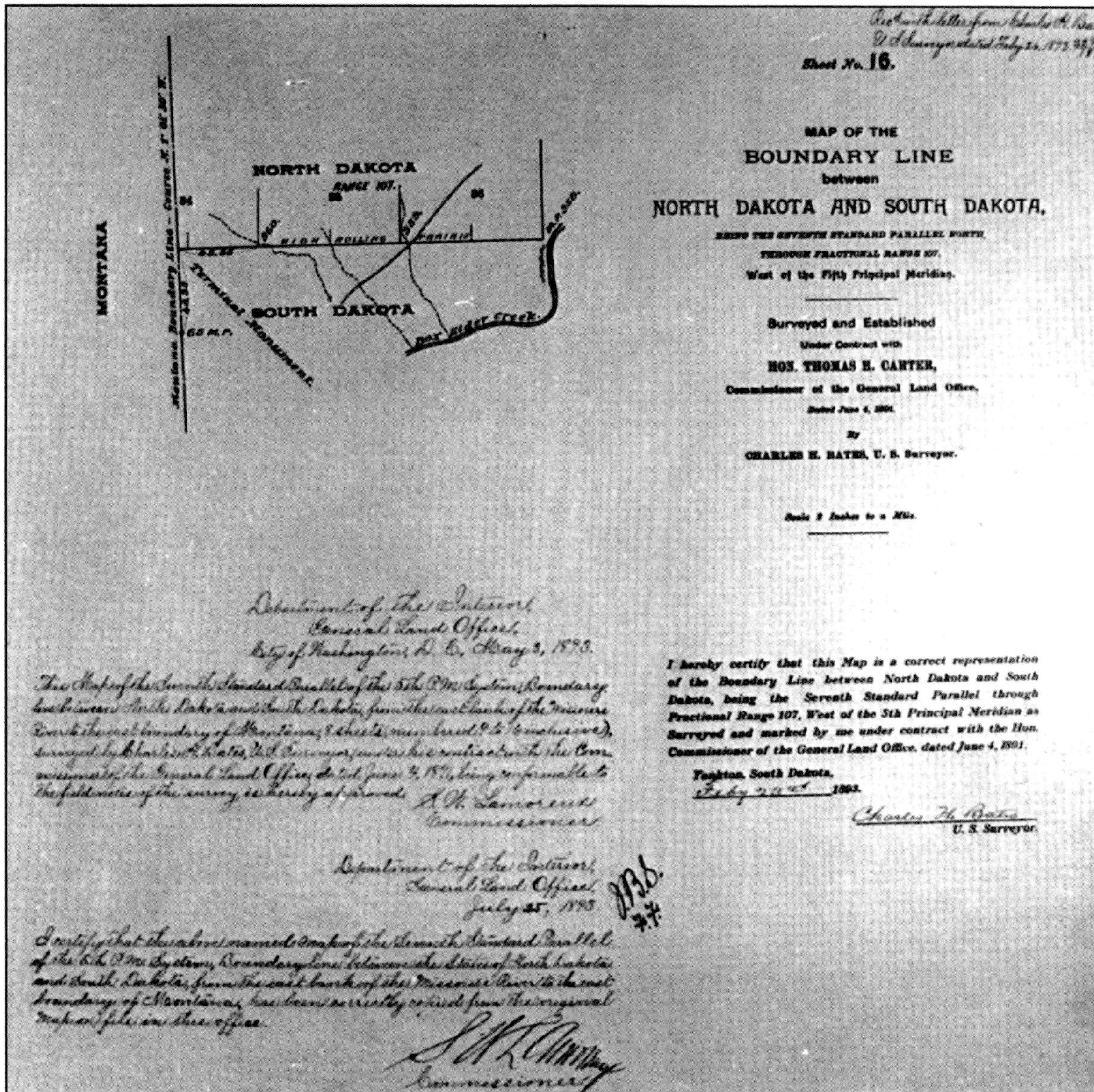

Sheet No. 16 of the maps of the boundary that Bates submitted with his field notes. According to the signed statement in the lower left corner, the maps agreed with Bates' field notes for that portion of the boundary between the Missouri River and the Montana border. They were, therefore, approved by the Department of the Interior on May 3, 1893. South Dakota State Historical Society.

in Marking" and referred to "certain irregularities or omissions in markings" that Beardsley had discovered in his examination. Markings on some monuments as recorded by Bates in his field notes did not correspond with what Beardsley had found in his examination. If the markings were as Beardsley had described them, Bates had to change his field notes to record "exactly" what the markings were. It was "one of the imperative requirements" of the General Land Office, Bates was reminded, that "field notes and work on the ground must correspond."

Beardsley's report noted only the following six errors or irregularities in the marking of the monuments, all east of the Missouri River:

> 12 mile corner (first mile corner inside the Sisseton and Wahpeton Indian Reservation), "S. C." omitted from the N. face of the monument.
>
> 16 mile corner (first range line corner inside the Sisseton and Wahpeton Indian Reservation), "T. 129," omitted from the N. face of the monument. There are also 6 horizontal cuts, or grooves, on both the E. and W. faces of this monument, which was a work the surveyor need not have put himself to.
>
> 17 mile corner. "T. 129" is cut into the N. face of this monument, which appears to be unnecessary, also.
>
> 35 1/2 mile corner. Has reversed "S" in "S. D." on S. face of monument.
>
> 37 1/2 mile corner. The characters "1/4 S. C." which should appear under "N. D." on the N. face of the monument, are omitted.
>
> 45 mile corner. This corner is evidently W. of the Reservation, as there are old mound and pits of the original survey at this corner. This monument has "S. C.", under "N. D." on its N. face; and 5 horizontal cuts, or grooves on the E. and 1 horizontal cut or groove on the W. face of the monument, which is extra labor.

Mile monument 16, set at a township corner where ranges 49 and 50 join. "T. 129" was left off the monument's north face, and six horizontal grooves were unnecessarily cut into the monument's east and west faces. Photo by the author.

These were all the irregularities Beardsley had found in the markings of the stone monuments. "They do not appear," he wrote, "to be very important; and it is a wonder there are so few among so many monuments."

Indeed, it is remarkable that so few errors had been committed in making the hundreds of markings on 720 monuments. But, for all his diligence, Beardsley apparently failed to note two errors, both on monuments west of the Missouri River, making at least eight errors in all.

Near Morristown, South Dakota, stands the monument marking mile 247 on which there is an error so obvious that Bates should have done something about it and Beardsley should have discovered it and commented on it. All numbers denoting the number of miles the monument was distant from the initial monument were to be placed on the *east* face of the monument. On this monument, however, the mile number appears on the *west* face of the monument, the only instance of this error on some 360 monuments bearing mile numbers. Making it even more unusual that neither Bates nor Beardsley noted the error is that a correction had been made in the number. The number had originally been "248," which was in error, so it was cut out and replaced with "247."

Just west of Morristown, and a short distance east of Keldron, South Dakota, another monument bears an error so obvious that it should have been noted by both Bates and Beardsley. On that portion of the boundary on which an original survey was being run (that is, across the Sisseton and Wahpeton Indian Reservation and along the entire line west of the Missouri River), half-mile monuments were to bear on their north faces the fraction "1/4" and the letters "S. C." in addition to the initials for North Dakota. On the monument marking the half mile between miles 252 and 253, the digit 4 of the lower part of the fraction "1/4" was omitted.

Bates made the changes in his field notes according to the suggestions that had been made in the first list. He answered the questions posed in the second list and requested that the necessary corrections be made on the plats that he had sent to Washington. To deal with the "Errors in Marking" contained in the third list, Bates had two alternatives. He could return to the field and correct the errors, which he offered to do, or his field notes could be corrected so that the written descriptions of the markings on the monuments matched the actual markings on them. He chose the easier alternative. Bates changed the wording of the field notes and provided an explanation for each of the errors.

Four of the errors, on monuments 12, 16, 17, and 45, were the result of a one-mile miscalculation in distance made at the time the monuments were marked at the quarry. The mistakes were not discovered until the monuments were on the ground, ready to be set. Monument 12 was prepared at the quarry to stand just east of the northern boundary of the Sisseton and Wahpeton Indian Reservation, when, in fact, it stands inside the reservation and should have

Mile monument 247 bears an error that neither Beardsley nor Bates noted. The mile number was incorrectly placed on the west instead of on the east face. The digit 8 has been replaced with the digit 7. Photo by the author.

The half-mile monument between monuments 252 and 253. The digit 4 of the lower part of the fraction "1/4" was omitted. This is another of the errors that neither Beardsley nor Bates noted. Photo by Curt Glasoe.

borne the letters "S. C." on its north face. The same error accounted for the unnecessary markings on the monument marking mile 45. Calculations at the quarry placed the monument inside the west boundary of the reservation, not outside. The same mistake changed the position of the monuments marking the township corners, accounting for the errors on monuments 16 and 17. Bates admitted to overlooking that the "T. 129," which was placed on monument 17, should have been cut *out* of that monument and cut *in* on monument 16.

Bates also explained the omission of the characters "1/4 S. C.," which should have appeared on the north face of the half-mile monument between monuments 37 and 38. He lacked one half-mile monument of the number necessary to mark the boundary within the Sisseton and Wahpeton Indian Reservation, so he was obliged to use one of those intended to mark the boundary outside the reservation, which were not required to have the characters "1/4 S. C." cut on them.

The "Reversed S" on the half-mile monument between monuments 35 and 36, Bates surmised, resulted from the quarryman's "getting his pattern upside down and thereby cutting the letter reversed." Bates chose not to make a correction on the monument because "to change this would deface the post more than to leave it as it is." (And, besides, the error is rather charming when one sees it on the monument.)

On March 25 Bates returned to the General Land Office by the Adams Express Company his original field notes, now corrected, of the survey of the boundary line between the states of North and South Dakota. Two days later, as a precaution against either shipment being lost, he sent the second and third copies. Bates hoped that the field notes would be satisfactory and that his explanations and corrections would be acceptable.

They were. On May 3, 1893, Bates received from the General Land Office what must have been a most welcome letter. "You are advised as follows," wrote the commissioner:

> Examination of the work in the field, and of the returns in this office, having shown that the survey has been executed in a faithful and honest manner, and in accordance with the terms of the contract and special instructions, said survey is hereby accepted, and the returns thereof are this day transmitted to the accounting division for final adjustment of the account.

When D. A. Ray, now chief of division "E" of the General Land Office, transmitted Bates' original field notes and a portfolio of sixteen maps to the chief of division "M" of the General Land Office on May 3, 1893, he wrote, "In justice to the Surveyor, Mr. Chas. H. Bates, early action on the account is requested."

For the modest sum of $21,300, United States surveyor Charles H. Bates had surveyed and marked "the most perfect and comprehensive boundary line in the United States."

The half-mile monument between monuments 35 and 36. The "reversed S" is the only instance of such an error in the thousands of figures that were cut into the monuments at the quarry. Photo by the author.

Chapter 8

The Monuments Today

"Until the heavens roll up as a scroll"?
Yankton *Press and Dakotan*

At the time that Charles H. Bates and the members of his survey party set the monuments marking the boundary between North and South Dakota, it was expected that they would stand forever, guarding the border like "silent sentinels on the prairie." References to the monuments suggested their massiveness, their durability, and their supposed permanence. They were referred to as "granite blocks holding down the line between the Dakotas," which would "defy the ravages of time until the heavens roll up as a scroll and the earth returns to its nebulous state." "From their size and weight," predicted the Winona *Times* on November 12, 1891, the monuments would "remain undisturbed until the time when we are called out of our graves to attend to the proceedings of the Day of Judgement."

Expectations, alas, have not been realized. The monuments have suffered at the hands of the elements, road builders, collectors, and vandals. Some, claimed by erosion and floods, lie covered with silt or water. Due to road construction, many monuments have been removed, later to disappear, or they have been buried in the grade. Inconsiderate individuals have removed monuments with which to grace their yards and drives. Unthinking people, some with the ubiquitous spray can of paint, have defaced others. With each monument that is removed, lost, or defaced goes a small part of Dakota history – and by that much is the integrity of the boundary between North and South Dakota diminished.

The initial monument, which should be accorded respect in keeping with its uniqueness, was nearly toppled when a large drainage ditch was dug near it. Local public-spirited citizens, assisted by the historical

A half-mile monument at the Railroad Museum in Wheaton, Minnesota. Photo by Corinne Iseminger.

society of nearby Wheaton, Minnesota, reset the monument, although not in its original location. The monument retained its pristine beauty until recently, when some individual, thinking to immortalize himself, painted his initials on each of the monument's four faces with green paint from a spray can.

Between the initial monument and the Sisseton and Wahpeton Indian Reservation, only one monument, number 4, remains standing. The rest were removed or buried when a road was built on the state line. Admittedly, the monuments would have presented a hazard to traffic had they been allowed to stand in the center of each intersection, but their loss is unfortunate. A half-mile monument, quite likely from this portion of the boundary, stands today in front of the Railroad Museum in Wheaton, Minnesota. Monument 8, removed during a road-widening project, lies in the grader ditch. Number 10 is buried in the driveway to a farmstead (I declined the farmer's offer of a spade with which to dig for it and thereby verify its location).

Many objects on the Sisseton and Wahpeton Indian Reservation are sacred, but not, apparently, monument 14. It was sacrificed when Interstate 29 was built across the boundary to bisect the reservation. Monument 17, one of those on which Beardsley found a marking error, no longer stands. It was set in one of the many "prairie drains" to which Bates referred in his field notes and has probably been pushed down and trampled under foot by livestock.

Monuments standing off the right of way and perhaps in the middle of a cultivated field no doubt pose a nuisance to farmers, even if they appreciate their significance and are willing to farm around them. Today, many monuments so located are nearly or completely buried by rocks that farmers have hauled from their fields. The monuments are protected by the rocks, but the effect is unsightly.

Disregarding decency and common sense, if not law itself, some people have removed monuments from their original settings and placed them on their own property. One half-mile monument stands embedded in concrete in Forman, North Dakota, a short distance from the boundary. Monument 51 has been moved to the lawn of a farmstead east of Havana, North Dakota. Number 56 was reset to stand beside the driveway into a farmstead, also near Havana.

On June 26, 1935, Orin G. Libby of the University of North Dakota History Department wrote to Russell Reid, superintendent of the North Dakota State Historical Society, regarding two of the monuments. President R. M. Black of the Industrial and Normal School at Ellendale had offered two boundary monuments, numbers 89 and 90, to the Historical Society. The monuments "were thrown out by the highway department" wrote Libby, and the Historical Society could have them for paying the freight on them from Ellendale to Bismarck. Reid agreed that the boundary monuments would make "a very interesting exhibit" in the society's museum and promised Libby that he would have the monuments shipped to Bismarck. They have since disappeared.

Mile monument 51 used as a lawn ornament on a farmstead near Havana, North Dakota. Photo by the author.

Mile monument 91 in front of the Great Plains Museum south of Mandan, North Dakota. Photo by the author.

Monument 91 now stands in front of the Great Plains Museum, which is located on the road between Mandan and Fort Lincoln in North Dakota. The museum's owner insists that the monument was purchased, but it is not clear from whom the purchase was made. Someone, apparently with a keen eye for proportion, has placed a monument on either side of the walk leading to the front door of his house in Garrison, North Dakota. The perfect balance is provided by monument 120 and a half-mile monument. Monument 128 stands in the shade of stately trees on a lawn in Ashley, North Dakota.

From Newark, South Dakota, to which monuments were shipped by rail in 1891, to some distance west of the James River, few monuments can be seen. A likely explanation is that they were removed or buried in the grade when a road was built on the boundary. Where the grade remains unimproved, the tops of some monuments can be found, level with the road's surface.

From a point near Lemmon, South Dakota, and continuing east for many miles is another long stretch where there are no monuments. Here, however, no likely explanation accounts for their absence. This is grassland. The monuments would not have posed a menace to livestock nor a hazard to farm equipment. What roads exist are unimproved prairie trails, so road construction is not an explanation. The monuments would have bothered no one had they been allowed to remain in place.

Despite their appearance of massiveness and indestructability, the monuments will break. The half-mile monument between miles 38 and 39, which originally stood beside a highway south of Rutland, North Dakota, was broken off when struck by the blade of a snowplow. For many years, the two pieces of the monument have lain just off the road beside a grain bin, discarded and forgotten. Number 169, broken off just below the surface of the ground when hit by a running horse, lies near Highway 83, a short distance east of the Missouri River. Other monuments have suffered the same fate, perhaps as the result of being struck by farm implements or because someone tried to remove them. The half-mile monument between miles 247 and 248 lies broken in two at the bottom of a ravine. Perhaps it tried once too often the patience of a rancher.

In his field notes, Bates recorded that his crew had set monuments on the banks of streams, on the faces of bluffs, and on the edges of steep ravines. Nearly a century later, many of these monuments have been claimed by floods and erosion. Monument 78, placed on the bank of the James River, is gone. Monuments 190 and 191, set on the east and west banks of the Missouri River, are probably lying beneath the waters of the Oahe Reservoir. Monument 357 and several half-mile monuments that Bates and his crew set near Box Elder Creek on the

Two monuments standing on either side of a walk in Garrison, North Dakota. Photo by the author.

western end of the boundary have also disappeared, having succumbed no doubt to the rush of the creek's current.

Just north of Pollock, South Dakota, Bates set monument 180 on the edge of a steep-sided ravine. As the sides of the ravine have been eroded, the monument has moved from the perpendicular and now juts horizontally into space. The same fate has befallen monument 181 which was set on the south face of a gravelly ridge. The monument points like an accusing finger in the direction towards which the water responsible for its indignity has rushed over the years. Monument 202 and the half-mile monument between miles 355 and 356 are among the most dramatic examples of those that have been claimed by erosion. Both were placed on the faces of high, steep bluffs and both lie today at the bases of those same bluffs.

Occasionally, monuments have been reset when road construction necessitated their removal. One such instance occurred at the point where Highway 65 crosses the boundary north of McIntosh, South Dakota. Monument 230 was moved instead of being buried. Someone's thoughtfulness is to be commended. When the monument was reset, however, it was oriented so that "S. D." is now on its north face and "N. D." is on its south face. Russell E. Kastelle provides a plausible explanation. When surveyors move a survey point, they indicate in some way that the point is no longer in its original location.

One could with good cause bemoan the loss of so many of the monuments to the human propensity for acquisitiveness, to thoughtlessness, and to erosion. But it would not do to end a discussion of the quartzite boundary on a despairing note. Large numbers of monuments, surely more than half of the original 720, still stand as

Mile monument 180 north of Pollock, South Dakota. Placed on the edge of a steep-sided ravine, it has nearly been toppled by erosion. Photo by the author.

Mile monument 181 north of Pollock, South Dakota. Water rushing down the gravelly slope has washed away the soil that once supported it. Photo by the author.

Mile monument 230 north of McIntosh, South Dakota, was moved because of road construction and reset to stand with "S.D." on its north face and "N.D." on its south face. Photo by the author.

The half-mile monument between monuments 355 and 356, lying at the base of a bluff in the Badlands after being toppled by erosion. Pieces of the rancher's fence are still attached to the monument. Photo by the author.

Mile monument 38 standing in a cultivated field on the Sisseton and Wahpeton Indian Reservation. The road in the background marks the section line. A conscientious farmer plows around the monument. Photo by the author.

Bates and the members of his crew set them nearly one hundred years ago.

Across the Sisseton and Wahpeton Indian Reservation, most of the monuments are in place. Due to the way this portion of the Dakotas was surveyed and settled, the monuments do not stand on the right of way nor on the section lines, so they were spared when roads were constructed. Property owners, for the most part, have respected the monuments and have not removed them, although many farmers have used the monuments as bases around which to pile the rocks they pick from their fields.

Along the southern edges of McIntosh and Emmons counties is another long stretch where most of the monuments remain in their original positions. Possible explanations for the large numbers of monuments to be found in this area are that much of the land along the boundary is used for grazing rather than for crop production, so the monuments are neither hazards nor nuisances to farm machinery; few miles of improved road have been built on this portion of the boundary, so the right-of-way is used for grazing and hay production – neither of which requires the removal of the monuments; and these areas of North and South Dakota were settled by German-Russians – thrifty, honest, hard-working people with a deep respect for authority and for things material.

Monuments also stand in regular sequence for some distance along the boundary just west of the Missouri River. Here are the breaks of the Missouri, and it may be the ruggedness of the terrain and the heavy growths of timber and underbrush as much as anything that have protected the monuments. This land is also under the jurisdiction of the Bureau of Indian Affairs in the Department of the Interior. Signs to that effect warn of the penalties for destroying or removing government property.

From White Butte, South Dakota, to the Montana line, few monuments are missing. Here the country is rolling, with an occasional high butte standing astride the boundary. From the tops of these buttes, one can look both east and west along the boundary through binoculars and see the monuments standing at regular intervals, very much like silent sentinels guarding the prairie.

Not only are many monuments still in place, they also continue to serve many purposes, beyond merely marking the boundary and guiding the wayfarer, which was what they were originally intended to do. When Bates had completed the survey and

The half-mile monument between monuments 134 and 135 south of Ashley, North Dakota. Here no road has been built on the boundary. The fences mark the limits of the right of way. Photo by the author.

Mile monument 258 near Thunder Hawk, South Dakota. The cant of the monument, the bare earth, and the tracks testify to the monument's use as a scratching post for livestock. Photo by the author.

Mile monument 286 marking a township corner and the point where ranges 94 and 95 join. The monument also serves as an anchor post for a fence and a pasture gate. Photo by the author.

marking of the boundary, he told the editor of the Sturgis *Weekly Record* that his having erected 720 superb cattle-scratching posts qualified him for membership in the Humane Society of the United States. Cattle still rub themselves against the monuments to get at that itch they cannot otherwise reach. Around many monuments their sharp hooves have cut deep, saucer-like depressions. On the treeless prairies, the monuments also serve as perches for birds, especially raptors.

Because the monuments were set half their length of seven feet into the ground, they stand solidly. Their massiveness and their being located on section lines make it impossible to resist the temptation to use them as anchors for fences on farms and ranches along the state line. The monuments are also handy posts on which to place "No Hunting" and "No Trespassing" signs.

Surveyors also use the monuments, as is attested to by the metal discs one occasionally finds affixed to them. Russell E. Kastelle, a surveyor in Breckenridge, Minnesota, uses the monuments as reference points when resolving cases involving property lines along the boundary. Landowners acknowledge that Bates "did an honest piece of work" and they appreciate the accuracy with which he set the monuments. Curt Glasoe, cadastral engineer with the Custer National Forest at Dickinson, North Dakota, has often found it more convenient to use a monument as a basis for bearing than to take celestial observations. Considering the instruments with which he worked, Glasoe once remarked to me, both Bates' survey of the boundary and his placement of the monuments are accurate to "a high degree."

More than those involved in surveying and marking the seventh standard parallel between North and South Dakota probably anticipated, the monuments are also useful because they bespeak the past. They speak

The terminal monument, marking the point where the boundary between North and South Dakota intersects with that of Montana. The distance between the terminal monument and the initial monument on the Minnesota boundary is 360 miles, 45.35 chains. Photo by the author.

of the public domain and the Ordinance of 1785 by which the land was surveyed and opened to settlement; they speak of a restless westering urge and the establishment of twin states where there was once

The west face of the terminal monument, bearing the name and title of the man who surveyed and marked the boundary between North and South Dakota. Photo by the author.

a single territory; they speak of the confident expectation that the unsettled portions of the Dakotas would be filled by eager home seekers who would find the marked boundary to be of "special utility" as they located their claims; they speak of budding industries in established cities like Sioux Falls and of high hopes for fledgling communities like Winona, White Rock, and LaGrace; and they speak of a vast expanse of virgin prairie across which people had to transport themselves and their goods by railroad, steamboat, and teams and wagons. Finally, the dates on the monuments serve as reminders that the two Dakotas are young states, only now celebrating their one hundredth birthdays.

There are few better places where one can identify with the history of North and South Dakota and be reminded of how recent that past is than at the terminal monument – where Charles H. Bates and his men ended their work on that hot August day in 1892 and where we end our discussion of the quartzite boundary.

The best way to approach the terminal monument, whether on foot or in one's mind's eye, is from the east. Start at the

Charles H. Bates (on the left) and a member of his survey party taken at the terminal monument in August 1892. South Dakota State Historical Society.

point where a nondescript road running south from Marmarth, North Dakota, intersects Box Elder Creek. Bates, with surveying experience in both Dakotas, had a high regard for this stream whose name belies both the swiftness of its current and the volume of water it carries. Stand on the creek's banks, as Bates must have done, and marvel at how the stream has torn its way through prairie and bluffs in its rush to join the Little Missouri River some distance to the northeast.

From the bridge spanning Box Elder Creek, it is a short walk of less than three miles to the terminal monument. If it is summer and if it has rained recently, the prickly pear will be in bloom.

At the terminal monument, one stands where Bates and the members of his survey party stood a century ago. Two of the men had their photographs taken while standing next to the monument. Content in the knowledge that they had done their job well, their faces wear expressions of self-conscious satisfaction.

A short distance to the southwest of the terminal monument, there rises a prominent butte. From the top of this butte, one can see for miles, far into the states of North Dakota, South Dakota, and Montana. And to the east, as beautiful as they were on the day they were fashioned at the quarry, one can see the magnificent monuments that mark Dakota's quartzite boundary.

Bibliographical Essay

Researching the surveying and marking of the seventh standard parallel that serves as the boundary between North and South Dakota was truly a pioneering effort, because almost nothing has been written about the project. In ten years of research, I have found only three references to it.

The earliest reference I found was in the 1897 edition of the South Dakota *Compendium of Biography,* in which a short essay on Charles H. Bates was included. Among the many accomplishments of Bates noted by the writer was his survey in 1891-1892 of "the best state boundary line in the United States," the one between North and South Dakota, a "fact that has been commented upon by many authorities upon this subject."

The second reference to the survey that I found was a single paragraph in the third volume of George W. Kingsbury's *History of Dakota Territory.* Kingsbury accurately described the monuments as being ten inches square and seven feet long, but he exaggerated their weight, which he gave as 1,200 pounds. He also erred when he wrote that the only markings on the monuments were the letters "N.D." and "S.D." on their north and south sides.

Almost fifty years after Kingsbury's *History of Dakota Territory* was published, the third reference that I found to the survey appeared in print. In his article "South Dakota Boundaries," published in *South Dakota Historical Collections* in 1964, Will G. Robinson devoted two and one-half pages to the boundary between North and South Dakota.

Robinson apparently based his treatment of the northern boundary of South Dakota on no more than a hurried reading of Bates' original field notes—one has to wonder if he ever saw one of the monuments. Robinson does refer to the monuments' having been quarried in Sioux Falls, South Dakota, but his descriptions of them and of their markings contain errors. He also included a brief discussion, not entirely accurate, of the difficulties Bates encountered when he attempted to locate the initial and terminal points of the seventh standard parallel on the Minnesota and Montana borders.

Apart from these three, short references, there is apparently nothing in print on the surveying and marking of the boundary between North and South Dakota. There is, however, a surprising amount of material in national, state, and local archives and in newspapers—especially South Dakota newspapers, because at the time of statehood North Dakota's twin had a greater population and in many ways was more settled and developed.

At once the most authoritative and most valuable material on the surveying and marking project are Bates' original field notes. As informative as they are interesting, the field notes were submitted to the General Land Office in Washington, D.C., in Bates' fine handwriting, as had been specified by the terms of his contract. Subsequently typed, the field notes are on file at the South Dakota State Historical Society in Pierre and are available on microfilm.

As required by federal law and by the terms of his contract, Bates recorded with painstaking care all natural and manmade objects that lay near the boundary, as well as the bearings and distances to them. He also included detailed descriptions of topography, soil, and mineral resources. To study Bates' field notes, therefore, is to acquire a knowledge of the geography of that portion of the Dakotas through which the boundary passes.

Second in importance only to Bates' field notes is the correspondence between surveyors Bates and George G. Beardsley and the General Land Office and the Interior Department in Washington, D.C. The original letters, instructions, contracts, bonds, affidavits, and final reports are preserved in the National Archives.

From the materials in the National Archives relating to surveying and marking the seventh standard parallel, one can conclude that the federal government took very seriously indeed all surveys of state boundaries and of the public domain. Instructions were explicit, even to where Bates' men were to place the excess earth from the holes in which the monuments were set

The archival material also reveals the inevitable bureaucratic red tape and the frustration that resulted from it. Both Bates and Beardsley waited impatiently for contracts and specifications without which they could not begin, continue, or complete their work. Nor was official Washington any more prompt in meeting its financial obligations in 1891-1892 than it is one hundred years later.

The Republican party in the presidential campaign of 1888 had made the reduction of the (sometimes politically embarrassing) treasury surplus an issue. The Republicans made good on their campaign pledge: the treasury surplus declined from $85 million in 1890 to only $9.9 million in 1892. The reduction was accomplished largely through greater expenditures – liberal pensions to Civil War veterans, for example – rather than by lowering tariffs or taxes.

For the first time since 1875, the same party controlled both houses of Congress and the presidency, and the Fifty-first Congress was one of the most active on record. Not without cause, it became known as the "billion-dollar congress." It spent more money than any previous peacetime congress in history. The existence of the treasury surplus and the Republican pledge to reduce it may have made easier Pettigrew's task of securing a federal appropriation of $25,000 with which to pay for surveying and marking the border.

The treasury surplus, notwithstanding, the materials in the National Archives suggest that the Interior Department and the General Land Office wanted to husband the funds entrusted to their charge. Both Commissioner Lewis A. Groff of the General Land Office and Acting Commissioner William M. Stone believed that a competent surveyor could be found who would run the survey and set the monuments for considerably less than the $25,000 that Congress had appropriated for the project. The secretary of the interior was nothing if not niggardly in suggesting the amount by which Beardsley was to be compensated for examining Bates' survey, and Bates had to wait until May 1893 to be paid for work that he had completed in November 1891 and August 1892.

Surveying and marking the seventh standard parallel between the two Dakotas was newsworthy, as were the efforts of South Dakota's enterprising Senator Richard F. Pettigrew to further his economic and political fortunes. Consequently, daily and weekly newspapers in both North and South Dakota are valuable sources of information.

Even when the newspapers are not indexed, a researcher possessed of pertinent dates and information regarding the survey can conduct a fruitful search. Bates was from Yankton, he had a contract to survey in the Black Hills in 1891, both Pettigrew and the quartzite monuments were associated with Sioux Falls – so the Yankton *Press and Dakotan,* the Sturgis *Weekly Record,* and the Sioux Falls *Daily Argus Leader* were logical newspapers with which to begin. Just as logical was the decision to read the weekly newspapers in the first tier of counties north and south of the state boundary.

Knowing the routes by which the monuments could be shipped to the boundary made it a simple matter to choose newspapers from the towns serviced by the Chicago, Milwaukee & St. Paul and Northern Pacific railroads. For the same reason, I read the newspapers from the Missouri River towns that would be most likely to report on steamboat traffic. I knew that both Bates and Beardsley traveled cross country – for example, from Yankton to the state boundary and from Dickinson to Grand Forks – and that they could cross the Missouri River only at Winona and Bismarck, so another group of newspapers from towns lying along these routes became a logical choice as possible sources of information.

Especially in the case of the weekly newspapers, the publisher more than likely was also the editor and the sole reporter. Consequently, he reported the news that was brought to him. Both Bates and Beardsley made it a point to stop at the newspaper office when they passed through a town. It is not to be imagined that they would be completely objective in the information they supplied. Pettigrew was his own best press agent, and he made certain that anything he did was cast in the best light possible when it appeared in print.

Making the boundary between the two Dakotas unique is the way that it was marked, not the way that it was surveyed. When he recommended C. W. Hubbard for the contract, Pettigrew pointed out that the survey itself was a simple exercise in land surveying. It was the marking that would require skill. Because the survey of the boundary had little to distinguish itself, therefore, I did not include much material on it. Nevertheless, some discussion of sources is in order.

Everett Dick's *The Lure of the Land: A Social History of the Public Lands from the Articles of Confederation to the New Deal* (Lincoln: U of Nebraska P, 1970) was the single, most helpful source of information regarding the surveying aspects of this study. Also helpful was a short, unpublished piece by Russell E. Kastelle entitled "Meridians, Base Lines, Parallels, Townships, Ranges and Sections in North Dakota." On the conditions that surveyors of the public domain encountered when in the field, I found valuable information in Zack T. Sutley's *The Last Frontier* (New York: Macmillan, 1930) and in two articles in *South Dakota Historical Collections* 5 (1910): Charles B. Clark, "Surveying on the Cheyenne" and Ferd J. Goodfellow, "South Dakota's Early Surveys."

Perhaps because Sioux Falls, South Dakota, was noted for the large quartzite deposits in the area and because high hopes were held out for the city's stone industry, a surprising amount of information is available on the material from which the boundary monuments were fashioned. Among the sources used are the following, listed in order of importance: Charles A. Smith, *A Comprehensive History of Minnehaha County, South Dakota* (Mitchell, SD: Educator Supply, 1949); *Something About Sioux Falls Jasper* (lavishly illustrated) published by the Hubbard Stone and Construction Company, Sioux Falls, South Dakota, in 1895; Dana Bailey, *History of Minnehaha County, South Dakota* (Sioux Falls, SD: Brown and Saenger, 1899); Rueben E. Bragstad, *Sioux Falls in Retrospect* (Sioux Falls, SD: Sanders Printing, 1967); the *Diamond Jubilee History of Jasper* (Jasper, MN: 1963); and Frank H. Hagerty, *The Territory of Dakota, 1889* (Aberdeen, SD: Daily News Print, 1889).

Pettigrew was a boomer for his state, for Sioux Falls, and for the city's industries—including the stone industry, so I used his papers in this study. Available in the original at the Pettigrew Museum and on microfilm at the Center for Western Studies in Sioux Falls, the papers have to be consulted for any topic dealing with territorial history, statehood, and Dakota politics.

Because the monuments had to be transported from the Sioux Falls quarry to points along the state boundary by the most economical means possible, I correctly assumed that Bates utilized railroads and steamboats. The *Travelers' Official Railway Guide, October 1892,* compiled and edited by W. F. Allen (New York: National Railway Publication, 1892) indicated the routes of the Chicago, Milwaukee & St. Paul and other railroads on which the monuments were shipped. William E. Lass in *A History of Steamboating on the Upper Missouri River* (Lincoln: U of Nebraska P., 1962) discussed steamboating on this major transportation artery. Many records of the steamboat companies operating on the Missouri River have been lost, but, fortunately, those necessary for this study have been saved. Bates shipped those monuments that were to be set west of the Missouri River from Pierre, South Dakota, on the steamer *Rosebud.* The dates, manifests, and charges were recorded in a ledger marked *Freight Book, Steamer Rosebud, Benton Transportation Company, 1891-1895,* deposited with the Baker Papers at the State Historical Society of North Dakota in Bismarck.

One cannot fully appreciate the difficulties associated with steamboating on the Missouri without knowing something about the characteristics of this remarkable river. For information about the "Old Mizoo," one can turn to Stanley Vestal's *The Missouri* (Lincoln: U of Nebraska P., 1964); and George Fitch's "The Missouri River, Its Habits and Eccentricities Described by a Personal Friend," *The American Magazine* 63 (1906-1907). For what has happened to the Missouri and many of the towns along its banks since the dams were built to tame the river, one can with profit consult Ray H. Mattison, "Report on Historical Aspects of the Oahe Reservoir Area, Missouri River, South and North Dakota," *South Dakota Historical Collections and Report* 27 (1954).

To add another fillip to my discussion of the surveying and marking project, I included descriptions of some of the towns that lay near or on the routes Bates and Beardsley would have traveled. White Rock, South Dakota, was a shipping point for the monuments and was Bates' base of operations on the eastern end of the boundary. To mark the town's centennial, Randy M. Olson wrote a history of White Rock and entitled it *Views of the Present . . . Visions of the Past* (Wheaton, MN: Gazette, 1984). The town of Winona, across the Missouri River from Fort Yates, and some of its better known residents were described by Ellen Woods and Euvagh

Wenzel, eds., *Emmons County History* (Linton, ND: Emmons County Historical Society, 1976). Much information on both Winona and Fort Yates can be found in United States, Record Group 94: *Records of the Adjutant General's Office, Medical Histories of the Posts in Dakota Territory,* "Fort Yates." Norman W. Cross discussed another of the many dreams that failed to materialize on the Dakota prairies in his article "New England City, Dakota Territory: A Narrative History, 1887-1912," *North Dakota History* 47 (1980).

For material on territorial history and politics and on the drive for statehood, I used the following standard works: George W. Kingsbury, *A History of Dakota Territory* 5 vols. (Chicago: S. J. Clarke, 1915); Clement A. Lounsberry, *North Dakota History and People: Outlines of American History* 3 vols. (Chicago: S. J. Clarke, 1917); William B. Hennessy, *History of North Dakota . . . including the Biographies of the Builders of the Commonwealth* (Bismarck, ND: Bismarck Tribune, 1910); *Compendium of History and Biography of North Dakota* (Chicago: Geo. A. Ogle, 1900); and *Memorial and Biographical Record, An Illustrated Compendium of Biography* [for South Dakota] (Chicago: Geo. A. Ogle, 1897). Most of these multi-volume histories are illustrated and contain biographical sketches of the subscribers to the works.

More recent histories of the two Dakotas have benefited from both research and perspective. Among those I used, the following were the most valuable: Elwyn B. Robinson, *History of North Dakota* (Lincoln: U of Nebraska P., 1966); Herbert S. Schell, *History of South Dakota* (Lincoln: U of Nebraska P., 1961); and Howard R. Lamar, *Dakota Territory, 1861-1889: A Study of Frontier Politics* (New Haven: Yale UP, 1956).

Also helpful were Lewis F. Crawford, *History of North Dakota* 3 vols. (Chicago: American Historical Society, 1931); Federal Writers' Project of the Works Progress Administration for the State of North Dakota, *North Dakota: A Guide to the Northern Prairie State* (Fargo, ND: Knight Printing, 1938; 2nd ed., New York: Oxford UP, 1950); and Federal Writers' Project, *A South Dakota Guide* (Pierre, SD: State Publishing, 1938). I also used two volumes in the Bicentennial History series: Robert P. Wilkins and Wynona H. Wilkins, *North Dakota* (New York: Norton, 1977) and John Milton, *South Dakota, A Bicentennial History* (New York: Norton, 1977).

Chance, more than anything else, led me to some nuggets of information. I learned from Robert 0. Parkinson's unpublished master's thesis entitled "The Early Career of Richard Franklin Pettigrew" (State University of Iowa, 1938) that President Benjamin Harrison used a pen made from an eagle quill with which to sign the proclamations of statehood for North and South Dakota. In Doane Robinson's *Encyclopedia of South Dakota* (Sioux Falls, SD: Will A. Beach Printing, 1925), I discovered that the town of Batesland in southwestern South Dakota was named after Charles H. Bates. I read about the weather that Bates could expect at the juncture of the Missouri River and the seventh standard parallel when he arrived there in November 1891 from *Resources of Dakota: An Official Publication Compiled by the Commissioner of Immigration* (Sioux Falls, SD: Argus-Leader Company, 1887). Fortunately for Bates, he put more stock in eastern weather forecasters than he did in publications that tried to entice people to come to Dakota to settle.

It remains to mention the government publications that were used in this study. Because the reasons for their use is obvious, they will be listed without comment: *Official Report of the Proceedings and Debates of the Constitutional Convention of North Dakota* (Bismarck, ND, 1889); *South Dakota Constitutional Convention* [July 1889] vol. 2 (Huron, SD: Huronite Printing); *Laws Passed at the First Session of the Legislative Assembly of the State of North Dakota, 1890* (Bismarck, ND; Tribune, 1890); *Statutes at Large,* 50th Cong., 2nd sess., 1887-1889, vol. 25; *Statutes at Large,* 51st Cong., 1st sess., 1889-1890, vol. 26; United States Congress, House, 51st Cong., 1st sess., 1889-1890, *Congressional Record,* vol. 21; United States Congress, Senate, 51st Cong., 1st sess., 1889-1890, *Congressional Record,* vol. 21; *United States Serial Set,* no. 2810, 51st Cong., 1st sess., 1889-1890, House Report no. 1080; *United States Serial Set,* no. 2812, 51st Cong., 1st sess., 1889-1890, House Report no. 1914.

Finally, *North Dakota General Land Office Plats* are on microfilm in the Elwyn B. Robinson Department of Special Collections at the Chester Fritz Library, University of North Dakota, Grand Forks, North Dakota. The plats that Bates drew of the boundary (on a scale of two inches to the mile) to accompany his field notes are located at the South Dakota State Historical Society in Pierre.

Index

The author at the Initial Monument.
Photo by Charlotte Iseminger.

The Author

Gordon L. Iseminger was born on a farm near Carthage, in Kingsbury County, South Dakota, and spent his childhood and youth on farms in Lincoln County. After serving two years with the United States Army in Korea, he received the B.A. in history from Augustana College, Sioux Falls, in 1959. He received the M.A. in history from the University of South Dakota in 1960 and the Ph.D. in history from the University of Oklahoma in 1965. Since 1962, Dr. Iseminger has taught at the University of North Dakota in Grand Forks, where he is professor of history.

Dr. Iseminger's family includes wife Trudy, a native of Germany, son Carl, twin daughters Corinne and Charlotte, and three grandsons and a granddaughter. A farmer at heart, he spends his spare time working in his garden and tinkering with Model A Fords.